Dream Road

Dream Road

XAVIER HERBERT

Illustrated by
RAY CROOKE

Foreword by
H. P. HESSELTINE

COLLINS

First published 1977 by William Collins Publishers Pty Ltd, Sydney
Type set in Monophoto Bembo by Asco Trade Typesetting Ltd, Hong Kong
Printed by Colorcraft Ltd, Hong Kong

ISBN *0 00 221593 4*

National Library of Australia
Cataloguing in Publication data
Herbert, Xavier, 1901–.
Dream Road.
I. Crooke, Ray Austin, 1922–, illus. I. Title.
A823.3

Again to sweet Sadie Norden whose love
for ever is my integrity

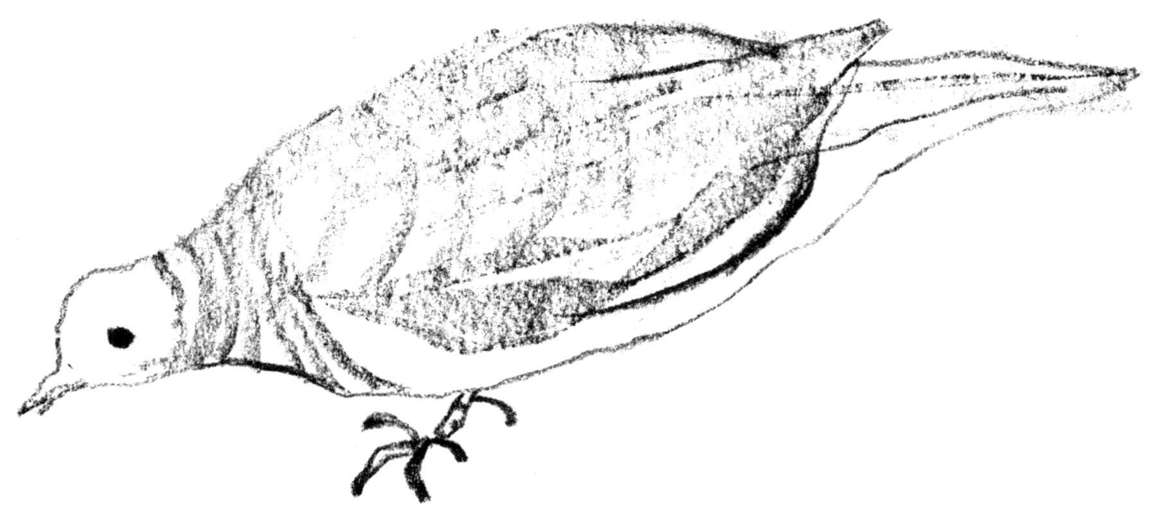

Editor's Note

FROM FIRST READING William Collins were overwhelmed by the great artistry of Xavier Herbert and his ability to create visions in the reader's mind. *Dream Road* is a series of these visions.

This book is the climactic chapter of 'Terra Australis', the first book of *Poor Fellow My Country*. Like many of the chapters in the complete book *Dream Road* is a monumental entity and inspired the eminent artist Ray Crooke to paint scenes from Herbert's country. The illustrations accompanying the text are the result of this inspiration.

Foreword

H. P. HESSELTINE

By simple word count, 'Poor Fellow My Country' is probably the longest novel ever written in English or any other language. By any sort of critical test, the book is not merely a massive achievement but a massively impressive one. Its main action spans something like seven years—from the accession of Edward VIII to the turning of the tide of the Pacific War after the Battle of the Coral Sea; its principal setting is the northern Australia that Herbert has made so peculiarly his own. The ramifications of the narrative, however, spread out to form a truly enormous pattern of implication. Scarcely a single event of importance in Australian or international affairs between 1900 and 1950 does not find its place in the complex network of Herbert's writing; hardly a public figure of any consequence is not accorded his appropriate recognition. *Poor Fellow My Country*, in fact, surveys and passes judgment on a half century's social, economic, and political history; in its continuous and confident traffic between history and invention it invites comparison with nothing so much as *War and Peace*.

At the heart of the book, however, is a fiction—a complex tale involving dozens of characters and defying easy summary. Not unnaturally, it also defies the ready isolation of representative passages. No single episode (or chapter even) could begin to suggest the disciplined abundance of Herbert's narrative powers, the extraordinary range of his human concerns. Certainly, the passage printed here can point to the full impact of the whole book no more adequately than any other. Some things, nevertheless, it points to very clearly, and these are among the basic building blocks with which Herbert had created the astonishing feat of literary architecture which is *Poor Fellow My Country*.

Dream Road tells of the pursuit of the adult Aboriginal King George and the halfcaste boy Prindy by Prindy's mother Nell and her tribal sister Peg-leg Queeny; in the telling it leaves no doubt of Herbert's magnificent gifts as a story-teller. An obvious *sine qua non* for a novel as long as *Poor Fellow My Country* is constantly exciting and varied action, and Herbert provides it in prodigal measure. Chapter after chapter is crammed with an excitement and suspense that are managed with a sureness that comes only from a lifetime's devotion to the story-teller's craft. The present passage, too, is representative in its bloody climax. Like *Capricornia* and *Soldiers' Women, Poor Fellow My Country* is thick with violence and death—tragic, comic, sheerly horrifying. Never before, however, has Herbert demonstrated more thoroughly the integral necessity of these images of blood and destruction to his artist's vision. For the novelist that he is, they constitute the irreducible metaphors for his understanding of man's fate. That fate, for Herbert, is founded on the inexorable resolution of many a seeming opposite or paradox—love and lust, free will and determination, magic and scepticism, religion and reason. Nell and George, Queeny and her dog—these do not die at a yarn-spinner's whim but at the behest of a creative artist for whom story telling is both an ungovernable need and a transfixing delight.

Dream Road traces out the converging routes of the two small parties, one male, one female, towards their fatal intersection in the land of the Frog Men, it instils not only a horrified awareness of impending human tragedy but also an overwhelming sense of the country itself—what Herbert has called again and again 'the spirit of the land'. His sense of the numinous in virtually every square inch of the Australian wilderness is not built on any Romantic mystification but on the most detailed, exact, and practical knowledge; among other things, *Poor Fellow My Country* is a handbook on outback survival. No white man has even written of the physical phenomena of the Australian land with a more remarkable fusion of passionate surrender to its beauty and expert understanding of its serviceability in sustaining human life. It is because most white Australians have disregarded the need for this literal closeness to the land itself that Herbert judges our civilization still to be profoundly alien to the continent it occupies. In this respect, *Dream Road* is profoundly representative of one of the most important and pervasive elements of *Poor Fellow My Country*: its aboriginality. At least into the 1930s and in northern Australia, Herbert argues, the tribal Aboriginals had the kind of preconscious affinity with the natural world they inhabited which makes for genuine culture, an affinity which is now lost as much to their detribalised descendants as to their white compatriots.

One urgent intention of *Poor Fellow My Country* is thus to enforce a vivid awareness of the culture of the tribal Aboriginals—through the creation of some remarkable characters, the depiction of their physical environment, the large scale explication of their elaborate religious mythology. Accordingly, the Ol' Goomun and Igulgul, the sun and the moon, are basic and recurring symbols in the novel, along with the other principal features of the creation myth centred in Koonapippi (also known as Kurrawaddi), the Earth Mother. One of the most notable figures in this mythology is Tchamala, the Rainbow Serpent, source and symbol of the diabolism which is accommodated into Herbert's version of Aboriginal custom and belief. Indeed, the painted galleries that George and Prindy enter at the beginning of the episode are the chief centre of the Cult of Tchamala. They venture on to this sacred and fearful ground only because the initiate George is introducing the novice Prindy to some of the more esoteric lore of the cult to which they both belong. The whole of their long trek through the wilderness is, in effect, a kind of initiation, in which Prindy is introduced to the secrets of the totem figure from the Dreamtime whom he virtually reincarnates. Such knowledge is strictly taboo to women, and George has therefore used a cruel trick to elude his two female companions. The force of Nelly's thwarted mother-love and of Queeny's long-standing hatred of George, however, overcomes all obstacles to the pursuit.

Herbert's respect for the magic, the pre-rational, in the Aboriginal sense of the word is writ large throughout *Poor Fellow My Country*—and most vividly in one of the great creations of the novel, Bobwirridirridi, the koornung or medicine man. Old Cockeyed Bob, released from prison by the amnesty proclaimed on the accession of Edward VIII, is, indeed, one of the motivating forces in the novel's entire action. His influence particularly casts its shadow over the halfcaste Prindy. At the opening of the novel, Prindy is a physically beautiful boy of some eight years old, already strangely withdrawn and notably sensitive to sounds and music. As the tale develops he becomes, as it were, the prize which some half dozen cultures and lifestyles struggle to possess. He is initiated, formally or informally, into Hinduism, Catholicism, Judaism, encounters Communists, policemen, squatters, bureaucrats. Only Bobwirridirridi, however, can divert him from following his own road towards identity. Under Bob's influence he is repeatedly initiated into varying stages of Aboriginal manhood. This lovely boy, potentially the prototype of all that might have been best in a different Australia, is in fact fought over, torn this way and that, in the end tragically destroyed.

Destroyed at the same time is Jeremy Delacy. In every way he offers a complementary portrait to Prindy. Jeremy is white where Prindy is coloured, old where he is young. He opts out of every convention as forcefully as Prindy is initiated into them. The bond between them, however, is closer than that of symbol or motif: Jeremy is Prindy's grandfather. The connection between the two is also developed through Jeremy's general concern for both the welfare and the culture of the Aboriginal people. In manifesting such a concern he is almost alone among the scores of white Australians who crowd the pages of *Poor Fellow My Country*. And the whole *congeries* of themes and attitudes associated with white Australians is probably that large aspect of *Poor Fellow My Country* most conspicuously not represented by the passage printed here. If white society is capable of a major virtue, it is probably the sort of sceptical rationality that Jeremy consistently displays. Few of his fellow white men, however, are depicted with anything like the same moral or emotional sympathy. Where Jeremy is independent, compassionate, deeply concerned for the maimed and the helpless, most of the other whites are self-seeking, convention-ridden, at once authoritarian and profoundly sycophantic. Such qualities attract Herbert's most intense scorn and disapprobation, sometimes satirical, sometimes undiluted and direct. A miserable race, we white Australians: having dispossessed a proud and cultured people, we remain content to be possessed ourselves by a race of absentee landlords—British or, later, American. No wonder we cannot tolerate a man like Jeremy Delacy, the 'scrub bull'; we must try in a variety of ways to destroy him.

If *Poor Fellow My Country* is, among other things, a large scale indictment of white Australian civilisation, the British and Europeans do not escape Herbert's contempt. Only the Jews, especially in the person of the beautiful refugee girl Rifkah, offer a pattern of life which commands anything like his full respect. Even the Jews, however, are aliens in Australia. Between all the white Europeans who find their way into the novel and the blacks are situated the unfortunate halfcastes. Herbert's treatment of their degradation and humiliation at the hands of the intruders has not abated one iota in acerbity since *Capricornia*. Further, the mere fact of their presence, the need to respond to them somehow or other, triggers a good deal of the action of *Poor Fellow My Country*. The entire inter-racial theme, however (like all else in the novel), is brought to a climax by the outbreak of the Pacific War. It is that war which Herbert sees, in retrospect, as both cause and symbol of the condition of Australia and Australians in the 1970s. For, in the end, his huge, complex, fascinating tale is as much an accounting with the way we live now as a cataloguing of events some quarter of a century old. The brilliantly unified control of its diverse actions, the graphic etching of its individual episodes, its cornucopia of unforgettable characters, its rich variety of feeling and tone: all these matters, I am persuaded, will recommend themselves in the strongest terms to formal criticism. But the reader who finishes *Poor Fellow My Country*, highbrow critic or anyone else, who fails to recognise in its title a *de te fabula* as well as an Aboriginal lament; who misses the savage assault on Australia here and now in the timeless work of the imagination—such a reader will be guilty of a major failure of moral sensitivity, and will mar what Herbert, in referring to his *magnum opus*, calls with some vehemence 'the honour of my purpose'.

At least as far as Njorjinga (also known as King George) was concerned, the trouble that put the runaways to flight again was much less the cause than the mere precipitant. He was fully prepared for it, not simply with all the necessities in the way of hunting appliances and other gear, but with assurance that their intentions should not be interfered with as before, through having these meet those of him supposed to be interfering at long distance, namely the Pookarakka back in Port Palmeston Jail. At first opportunity for privy male talking, George told Prindy he had made up a Letter Stick for sending to the Wise One, to say that they two would be going on to the Alice Country to await his coming when he freed himself. The message had been entrusted to one of the Hang On Creek blacks, who would be going in to Town with Nugget Knowles. He and Prindy would take the two women as far on their way to the Beatrice as need be for them to find the rest of it themselves, then desert them. They couldn't be mixed up with women in the bijnitch ahead of them. Mt Mooragetaghee was their immediate goal. They must reach it this first day, going by ridges to avoid leaving tracks for police. Once there they would have the advantage of the magic it offered. Climb to the top, and not only did you have a view of the country from sea to sea, but a hint of all that would be happening to concern you during this period of Igulgul. Then there was its stock of brush-tail wallabies. They would be wanting a couple of tails for their subsequent journeying. There were also the porcupines: 'Aw, mek'm spit come out!' said George, swallowing his saliva.

George chanted the legend of Mooragetaghee, the Echidna (or Porkypine to ignoramuses):

Burragin ga burragin
Widji getigheenya Mooragetaghee, Mooragetaghee,
Wudda baddah, wudda, baddah, wudda baddah. . . .

Prindy joined in which a version of his own, despite the scolding of his mother and the mockery of his aunt Queeny:

Ol' Mooragetaghee, minji long o' water he.
Brolga come an' up him bum shove him spear . . . he he!
Proper minji bugger dat one Mooragetaghee—ee-ee!

The legend told of how Mooragetaghee was camped on a waterhole in dry country, when along came the Brolga People, very thirsty. Too mean to share the water, Mooragetaghee got on top of the hole and covered himself with mud, to make it look as if the hole were dry. The Brolgas said, 'There may be water down below. Let's try with our spears.' They all dug their spears into Mooragetaghee, who leapt out and fled, with the spears still sticking in him. He was crying to himself about the spears, when Wanjin the Dingo came along and offered to pull them out. But Mooragetaghee didn't like the way Wanjin was slobbering, and said, 'No thank you. I'd rather have spears in my back than myself in your belly.' Thereupon he dug himself into the ground; and the spears grew into the quills his descendants carry to this day. Likewise to this day do porkypines dig themselves in with amazing facility to avoid other creatures. Mt Mooragetaghee, or Finish, is where the Old Porkypine dug himself in for the last time, piling up a great heap of dirt and rock to mark the spot.

All that day they had glimpses of the fabulous mountain, seeming by their round-about-going to get no nearer, so that Queeny, toiling on stump and crutch, trying not to leave tracks, in extremes of thirst and fatigue and complicated belief, got the idea that she was being led a dance by what she called no-goot blackfeller bijnitch, and yelled about it. Through Prindy, King George replied that those who didn't like it could go back. She tried an old blackfellow trick of shortening hard travel by Singing the destination nearer, but did it to the tune of *Jesus Loves Me* and in Jesus's name: 'Jesus bring him dat place close, 'fore I knock-up, Jesus, please. . . .' Nell might have been in it too, the way her lips moved. George whooped with merriment in telling Prindy how much notice that Old Mooragetaghee was going to take of Jesus Bĭjnitch.

Still, it was as if by magic of some sort that, in the vermilion and silver evening, from seeming to have lost Mooragetaghee altogether since the Sun went down behind a high intervening ridge, they topped the ridge to find him right before them, no more just a bit of peeping blue, but a mass, deep green and silver, very much like the bulk of a sleeping giant animal. The magic of it, like an emanation of its moon-silvered scales of rock, warm and iridescent, enveloped them as they went on down to the dark foot of it, causing Queeny to cry out that she wasn't going any closer. But George had been telling Prindy of the sweet water they would find tumbling from those rocks. She stopped only long enough to utter a fervent prayer: 'You look out me, Jesus . . . I you goot girl, Queeny'.

The Shade of Mooragetaghee led them straight to water, to a winking pool fed by a streamlet tinkling out of granite that seemed to glow. Sweet sweet water! They sank sighing on to silky couch-grown sand. It was George said they were under the patronage of the Old One, directed by another, the Master, at the moment staring out of one red eye, as if he, Tchamala, were leaning over the silver wall of rock towering above them. Queeny must have her say, exhausted or not: 'Don' you believe dat, boy. Dat one heye belong Bible God. He lookin' out for you and me and my tchister . . . but no-more lookin' out rubbitch blackfeller.'

'Dis blackfeller country,' said George to Prindy. 'Too much *moah* for whiteman dis place. Anybody talk whitefeller way here get sick.'

'Yuuuurh!' commented Queeny, but nevertheless shut up.

According to knowledgeable whitemen, the red eye would be the planet Mars. George, the ignorant blackman, called up to it in lingo, while the others stared. Surely eye winked in reply! George told Prindy that he had informed the Master that they would be climbing to the top tomorrow and would be wanting a couple of rock wallabies.

'You no goin' up dere.' said Nell to Prindy. He ignored her.

That the place abounded with brush-tails was made evident when they had their fire going and the creatures, bold in their magical advantage over common intruders, came leaping down over the rocks to a take a look, not to be seen, since they were silver-grey like the rocks themselves, but to be heard, bounding, slithering, sending the small stones scattering. 'Cheeky bugger,' said George to Prindy. 'He don' savvy me-two-feller Tchineke Man.'

'My boy not Tchineke Man,' snapped Nell.

George chanted a bit of Snake Man stuff; and Prindy echoed him.

Poor Mungus, tied up, was squeaking with excitement, and not only because of the wallabies. There was scuffling and squeaking and rustling all around them. A particular sound, a sort of sighing and clicking, made, so George said, by porkypines. They would leave them till tomorrow night, when they would have a rock over prepared for cooking them: 'Aw mek'm spit come out!'

For supper they had bread and beef and tea. Then they settled down to sleep—while smirking Igulgul sailed towards the wall of rock behind which the Eye of Tchamala had vanished. Igulgul had just taken his last look and slipped behind the mountain, leaving a weirdly glowing darkening world behind, when Prindy began to sing *La Golondrina*. It was rather different from any other of these odd outburstings of his spirit, probably by reason of the conditions of the moment. Queeny and Nell reached for each other and lay tense while it lasted; and Mungus lifted up his head and sobbed quietly in chorus. A hush fell even on the scuffling creatures. Only George seemed to be undisturbed.

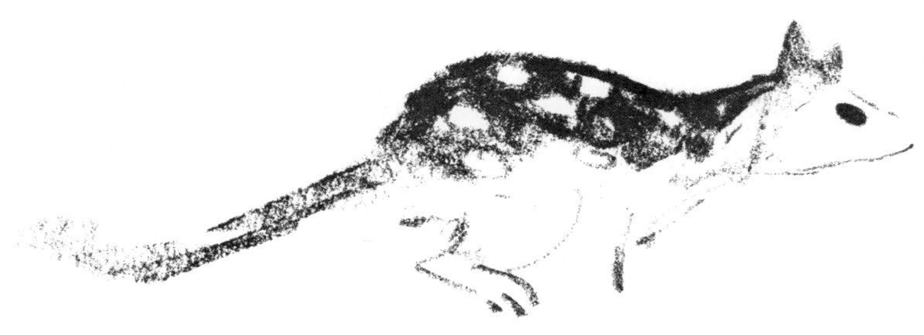

18

George and Prindy were up at dawn. The women just took a quick look at things in the ruddy twilight, then buried their heads in their sacking bedding. Drinking tea with bread and beef, George remarked on the abundance of vegetable food thereabouts, yams amongst the rocks, some tall palms with hearts the length of your arm, cycad nuts for making nut-bread; stuff for women to collect, unless they wanted the men who hunted meat for them to do what Gurrawirrilyama, the Butcher Bird, did to his lazy-bone mob. No response from the sacking. But when George said that they would be off up the mountain, Nell sat up, saying sharply, 'You stop here, boy!'

Prindy looked at George, who looked aloft, saying that he was an old and broken-winded man who might die up there; and who then would lead the party to the Beatrice; and if he didn't go up, how were they to know who might not be following them or plotting to waylay them? Then turning his back completely, as a brother should when forced to address his sister directly, growled, 'Spone you no more let him my boy do it properly way long o' him huncle . . . den, all right, I leave him you . . . bugger you . . . you look out yo'self!'

Nell was silent, George waited a moment, then reached for his hunting gear leaning against a tree, and said to Prindy, 'All right, *Kokanjinni* . . . You come.' Prindy leapt to his own small weapons.

The only one to express any more concern about their going was Mungus, still tied up, and sobbing broken-hearted. As George had said, if he went with them he would run straight into the jaws of a python.

Prindy would have gone up over those shiny grey rocks like the brush-tails who kept them polished, and indeed did so till the waste of energy dawned on him after several trips back to sit with George while he recovered breath or to take his gear while he scrambled up pinches needing the strength of both his old hands. There was no sign of the riotous life of the night before. The wallabies would be in their nests asleep now, in nooks and crannies in sheer rock faces inaccessible even to the rock pythons, who would have to depend on the wind spirits to locate the sleepy beasts for them so that they might lie in wait when they emerged heavy with sleep in the cool of the afternoon.

It all went back to the magic dispensed by Tchamala and Mooragetaghee. The pythons were keeping out of sight, too, not because they were sleepy, their kind getting that way only after a huge meal, but from fear of Old Wátagarra, the Wedge Tail, sailing up there in the violet, so easily, so peacefully and minding his own business, it would seem but all ready to drop out of the sky like a stone and strike dead with a blow of his mighty shoulder anything worth his while that moved. One thing did move, disturbed by the intruders, that must have filled the eagle with chagrin enough to come down to take it out on them, only for their spears. It was a large python, the best of twenty feet in length, with a couple of bulges in its middle that wouldn't have gone into a bran-sack. As it went sliding awkwardly down a steep slope of rock, George called to it, 'No-more fright, Jullungall . . . me-two-feller Tchineke Man!' The huge snake, with blue tongue flickering to pick up the sound, looked back as if in acknowledgement, then slid over the lip of the rock, the last of him running in a cleft between two rocks, like a sluggish stream of oil-streaked water, rainbow-hewed in the blaze of the Sun. George remarked, 'Spone dat old feller Watagarra up top dere been gitchim dis one, he can call up all-lot him mate, mek him properly *beeeg* tucker.'

It was a good thousand feet to the top. At last there they were, with the Wind Spirits jostling them and whispering around them, and with all the world laid out before them, north-west, south-east, as a blackfellow counts, needing but two points to his compass, those from which blow the prevailing winds. Northwest a serpentine silver ribbon wound through emerald vegetation to the silver sea that stretched away to China. That was what the *kuttabah* called the Finish River, but was really the track made by Mooragetaghee when he came up from that hole he'd made when the Brolgas had filled him with spears. The hole was that bay of mud where they had been shipwrecked. So George informed Prindy as they looked around the world. Away west-west of North lay their ultimate destination,

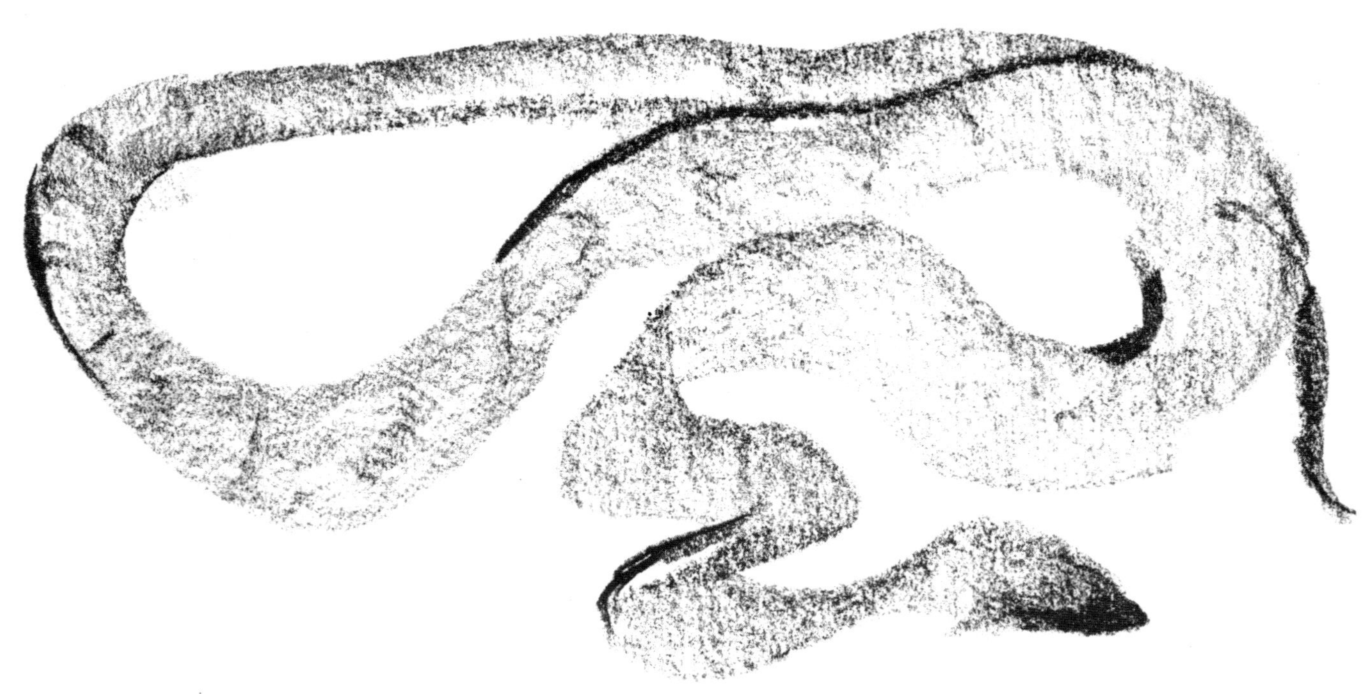

the Alice River Country. East-east of South was a shimmer of silver below the blazing blue, which was reflexion of the waters of Port Palmeston. South-south-south of East they followed a line of dust that obliterated the horizon that was the continent. George reckoned the dust was raised by the whitemen building the new road. As they watched they saw a pillar of the dust rising like a willy-willy, but was not made by frolicsome spirits of Tchamala's mob, as true willy-willies are, instead by whitemen, as evidence the faint *poom*! they soon heard from it. 'Dynamite,' said George. 'Whitefeller he don' like nutching in way. He got 'o blow-him-up.' Prindy asked could the *kuttabah* blow up Mooragetaghee. 'Can't do dat,' said George. 'Too-much *moah*, dis place. Whitefeller fright'. Das wha' for he call-yim Finish, I reckon.'

George listened to the Wind Spirits, and said they told him no one was following them, but they got to look out more far dat-a-way—he indicated due South: 'Might be trouble sumpin' . . . we got 'o look out. Come on, we go now. Wind him tell him which way we gitchim brush-tail.'

Ostensibly under occult direction then, George found the spot, one so obvious that anyone less conversant with the Laws of Nature might well have done it alone. It was about halfway down. Two huge bulbous boulders, joined to look like a giant's buttocks, lay beneath a sheer wall in which, some fifteen feet above the gluteal humps, just a nice hop-up for a rock-wallaby, was a ledge so well polished as to betray for certainty the cubby holes behind it. Likewise was the giant's posterior polished. As it was impossible from below to see anything behind the ledge, so was it from above to see anything below that didn't stand well clear of the base of the humps. Not that that would trouble a brush-tail, which dropping down into a dangerous situation, could as easily bounce up out of it. Hence the need for magical assistance. The next step was to sit under cover and out of range of super-sharp hearing and scenting, Singing Marmaroo out to do the silly things he must to die on the end of a spear.

Blue shadow rolled down the mountainside, to fill the gully below and rise up to the further ridge. The south-easter swept up against it, as wind over contrary tide, tossing the grass and scrub and a cloud of finches, and bringing with it the hint of smoke from the camp below. Everything to suit the strategy. Now was the time, said George, in response to windy advice giving in little moans and whines and whispers. They came out crawling to the base of the boulders, there to part, Prindy to go on hugging the rock to the windward side, George to stay. George had said that when the wallabies dropped down they would turn windward because of the smell of smoke and would pick up that of Prindy, and go warily to that side to take a look. They wouldn't be able to see him, but would know he was there. Bold as they were, one would try jumping over him to the rock beyond. He was to be ready with his spear to hit it in the belly as it went. No matter if he missed. The others would come the other way, and must land on a great flat slab where they would be sitting targets.

Thus it turned out. Soon half a dozen blackish heads were seen peeping down. Then as many furry forms flying through the air. A few minutes of tense waiting. Then a whitish belly flying over Prindy—*phwit*! The spear flew, struck with an audible thud. The little grey beast, woolly with winter coat, landed on a big sloping rock, tangled with the protruding spear, fell, to go skidding and clattering out of sight. Prindy stood. Then a call: '*Yu*!' He ran out, saw George going towards a thrashing bundle on the slab on

his side, and other grey forms high-leaping far away. Then he ran round the other side of the big sloping rock. There lay the other victim of magic and primitive coordination of human hand and eye, killed by itself, in fact, through falling on the small spear that could have done little more with a boy's strength behind it than penetrate its hide, so that it was driven clean through. The stricken little animal lay on its side, with stream of blood pouring from the creamy belly, quivering, blue tongue licking at the sand. It raised its head slightly, to regard the boy with great dark eyes that seemed full of astonishment at his nearness. A tiny struggle. Then the eyes glazed, the head fell back. 'Poor bugger.' murmured the hunter, and bent and heaved it up, hooked an arm under its haunches, and with the head dragging on the ground, went back round the rock. George, looking, cried, 'Yakkarai . . . number-one strong womera-man!'

With string torn from a little hibiscus bush they tied each of their victims, hind foot to tail tip, thus making a loop to go over the shoulder. Then they went down. The Sun was down, Igulgul halfway up the sky, floating like a silver boat in a sea of vermilion. Butcher birds were singing at the camp for their expected breakfast. The air was sweet with the savour of roasting yams. Nell greeted the hunters with a tirade of abuse that surely expressed the anxiety she had been feeling for one of them, to be silenced by that one himself, flinging his share of the spoils at her feet, saying, 'Liver . . . you wan' him, eh, Mumma?'

They had grilled liver and roast yams to sustain them till the anticipated feast of porkypines became a reality.

Preparation for the feast had to be made with the firing of a ground oven, and for the hunting with the gathering of small termites' citadels and scraps of grub-ridden wood. These latter were scattered in a cleared space just off rocks where judging by last night's sounds echidnas abounded. Saplings were also cut for what were called crow-bars, which would be the only weapons used. It was truly night by the time everything was ready, and the porkypines on the move again. Then the entire party went to the clearing, to squat on the edge remote from the rocks. George, Prindy, and

Nell had crow-bars. Queeny sat with Mungus on a lead. All that was required of them was to step lightly.

The echidna, invulnerable to all predators but man, evidently lives in constant fear of his single enemy, listening always for his tread, upon hearing which he freezes into what looks and feels like a lump of stone—if you're smart enough to get to feel him before he does that disappearing trick of his. He never moves in the open if he can help it except where the earth is soft and he can utilize his almost magic facility for digging himself into it. Digging under himself like a machine and with the strength of a machine, he can vanish before one's eyes and make a day's work for anyone fool enough to let things go to such a pass that he has to be dug out. Only a man can dig him out. Only on account of a man will he dig himself in. Only a man knows that his is the sweetest of all meats—a man and those creatures wise enough to wait on men's scraps, like those butcher birds clucking in anticipation up in the trees.

It wasn't long before the long snouts in amongst the rocks picked up the scents of termites and wood-grubs, and the weird sighings and clickings were converging on the little clearing. Then one appeared, an old-man who'd take up the best part of the space of a 70-pound sugar-sack, looking like a round ant-bed, black as shadow, save for a glint struck by the moonlight from his myriad little flat-lain spines. He waited, snuffling and clicking, full of suspicion for the moment. Mungus, in Queeny's powerful grip, nearly had a fit with stifled excitement. One yap escaped him, but apparently made no difference to the old fellow, who came on, shuffle-snuffle, following his nose. It must have been his assault on the bait that brought the others, the sound of his crunching, the odour of those delicacies that, although surrounded by them in profusion, they were limited in partaking of because of their suspicion of open spaces. There were seven of them on the pile when George gave the sign to get ready.

George had said that there was only one way to deal with them, which was to pounce with the crow-bar and roll each one over on his back and settle him with a whack on the belly. It must be done in a moment. Once he started to dig in you would never get the stick underneath him, because he would throw it out with his churning iron claws; and it was useless striking him on the mailed back. Invulnerable as he was otherwise, he was so vulnerable about the belly that a single blow would kill him. The pity was that Mungus hadn't understood the instructions. But then, being a *mungus*, he would have to learn the hard way.

George gave the signal *go*! The three leapt to it—and Mungus too, with so much strength despite his size, that he dragged Queeny to her feet without her crutch, hauled her reeling into the fray. Quite naturally, poor Mungus attacked his beast with his teeth—and got the shock of his life, yelped piercingly as the spines struck him in the nose, turned howling, swung round Queeny's peg, spun her, so that she fell, big bottom down, on top of the same heap of prickles, or at any rate as much as still remained above ground, which was quite enough to make her shriek at the top of her terrific voice. They got only four, the style of the three with the crow-bars being cramped not only by the mix-up but by the mirth it caused them. For minutes they were helpless with laughter.

The laughter went on, in bursts of giggles that worked up to shouts, throughout the couple of hours of cooking. Even Queeny joined in it after a while, and Mungus, and the butcher birds.

Seeing that one of the bag was that old-man porkypine, there was a good enough feed with the four. Those who hadn't so far tasted meat of the kind, the inlanders, mother and son, agreed that it was properly tweet-one, tweet-one, the best they had ever tasted. Igulgul was gone over the mountain before they went to bed. Perhaps it was the rich food that caused Queeny to dream again, still of the flying fox trying to take her. She woke screaming, 'You black bastard . . . you try kill him me, I kill him you!' She was upset even more than last time, so that it was a couple of hours before they were able to settle down again.

II

They stayed on at Mooragetaghee till Igulgul had passed his fullness and there would be less likelihood of meeting that threat ahead of them; or so said George, who was still troubled about what the winds had whispered. He and Prindy went aloft to check on that. It was still away there—southeast or southwest, it was hard to tell. 'Can't mek it out,' said George. 'Nutching belong 'o Old Man.' He showed he was referring to Bobwirridirridi by jerking his jaw east-east-northward. 'Deveren kind trouble.' According to Queeny, the scoffer at blackfellow logic, the real trouble was that the hunting was good and that a bloody blackfeller was having a blackfeller holiday at the expense of the discomfort of civilized people. There might have been something in what she said, because George and Prindy were out every day hunting, and George was evidently happy to be practising the ancient skills again and teaching them to an eager pupil. The hunting was all that could be desired, so much so that much of the game was spared after being stalked for the joy of it: great kangaroos, emus, brolgas. The western side of the mountain was climatically quite different from that where they were camped. Sheltered from the harsh winds of Dry Season, it was largely grown with rainforest. Here were jungle-fowl and a camp of flying foxes. It was from this side that the Finish River had its beginnings in swampland as prolific in bird life as the billabongs of Lily Lagoons. Duck, goose, bustard, quail, yabbies, mussels, catfish, and always a porkypine or two, were hung about the camp, ready for tossing into the ground oven whenever anyone felt hungry, to be eaten with great cakes of cycad nut, which though it stank after fermentation in water so that all the blue-bottles in the country came to camp with them, was so tasty as to be hard to leave alone. Along with the flies came the crows and the rest of the butcher bird population, and a couple of kites—to the perverse amusement of that old eagle, who sometimes swooped low over the crowded trees just to give the feathered bums a fright.

The women had really little to complain of, but so little to do as to need to complain. It was useless telling them they were loafers like the birds cawing and clucking and whistling around them and had never had it better, as George frequently did through his medium for talking to them, because

their answer was that they were not bloody blackfellers and wanted to be on their way to the Beatrice and the civilized things belonging to it that became more and more alluring as talked about.

How long it might have gone on was anybody's guess, considering the pigheadedness on both sides. Anyway, it ended quite suddenly, even shockingly, by reason of what seemed to be involved, the cause of it an old-man goanna, of the large spotted rock kind, a *prindi*, called Warradabil by George.

The creature had been seen about for a couple of days, having come to join the feasting with the other bush scavengers. No one had molested it, because it was Prindy's Dreaming Mate and could not be killed without his permission, which he wouldn't be able to give unless the others were in real need of food. Mungus had had a go at it, but only to get a good fright when the three feet or so of its scaly white belly and throat reared over him, with claws extended and what looked like a hundred sharp teeth bared, and then to get a cuff from Prindy and lecture on the ethics of the thing. He repeated what George had said, that Warradabil might well be Prindy's dead Daddy's Shade, called *Lamala* in western lingo.

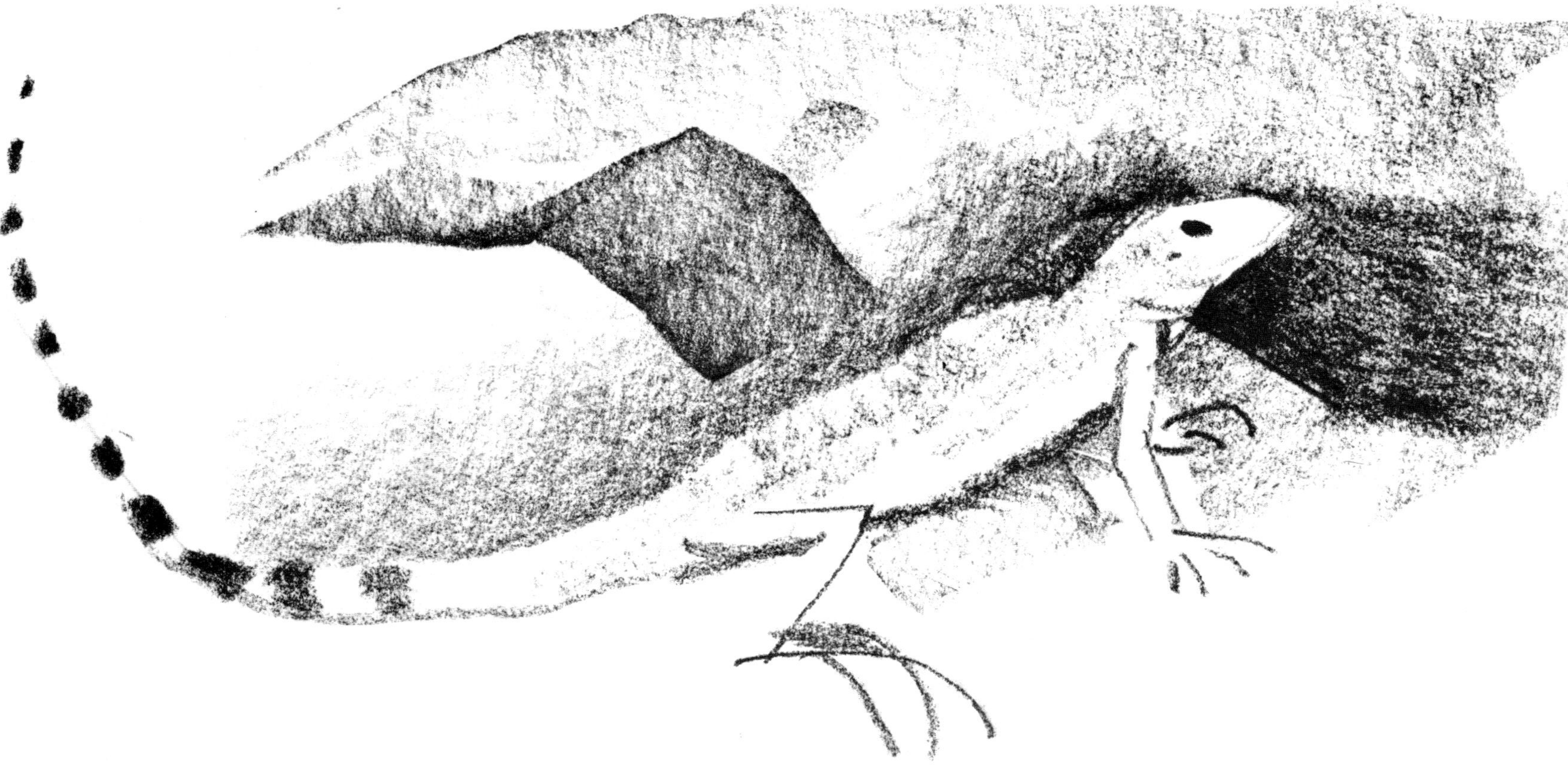

The birds were interested in the goanna only as a rival, he being much too big and ferocious a thing for any of them to tackle even in a gang . . . that is to say the feathered scavengers. For there was that other, the eagle, Watagarra. The great bird would know everything that was going on below and be biding his time. Then there he was, that morning, hurtling down over the rocks in a dive. The scavenger birds saw him and gave the alarm. The goanna, well out in the open, started a bee-line for the rocks. But it happened that Queeny was sitting on a rock just there, and not knowing what was going on, thought the huge lizard was attacking her, and leapt up with a yell and struck out with her crutch. But only lightning or an eagle could hit a goanna really on the run. With all that wood about her, he must have thought Queeny was a tree, and needing the first cover he came to, shot up her, hung for a moment staring into her face with talons hooked in her breasts, while the eagle went over. Then with her shrieking and spitting right onto the long forked tongue he was listening with, and her pounding his armoured back with the head of the crutch, he was moved to shin up further, grabbed an ear and a loop of her knotted hair, and there he was sitting on top of her head, forepaws extended and head turning from side to side, as if delivering a lecture, horny tail round her neck for better support. The three people watching whooped with sudden laughter. The birds took it up. Mungus barked. Queeny shrieked, 'Tek him 'way, tek him way . . . kill him!' But the others were helpless.

Now the goanna was watching his baffled foe spiralling aloft. Then Queeny raised the head of her crutch and started beating with it wildly. The goanna grabbed it, probably thinking it a limb of the odd tree, shifted onto it, and as it fell with his weight, came down in swift arc, to land on his back on a slab of rock with the crutch on his belly. He lay jerking, with the wind knocked out of him.

Queeny raised the crutch, screeching, 'You bloody bastard!'

George yelled, 'No-more!'

Prindy gasped, 'Don' you, Aunty!'

But with all her considerable strength she brought the crutch down and caught him in the side just as he was rolling over. Again he fell back winded.

'Eh! Eh!' yelled George and Prindy.

But she pounded the stricken creature with a succession of swift sharp strokes, so that his belly opened up and guts and blood came bursting out. With a mighty contortion he gained his feet, shot for the rocks again, reached them, went clawing up, got his trailing entrails caught on a projection, heaved himself round to get clear. Again the birds gave the warning. The great head came up. He tried to run for it. But there was Watagarra with great wings out to brake his dive and the wind whistling through them and talons outflung to grab. *Swish*!—and there was poor old Warradabil, with guts trailing behind him, having his first flight.

No laughter now. Even the birds were silent. Prindy, looking up, muttered, 'Poor-feller, my mate!'

Then George turned on Queeny, as a brother is entitled to in extremes of bad behaviour, and roared, 'Wha' for you do like o' dat, you bloody cranky rubbitch?'

'Shut yo' bloody puggin' mout', you black bastard!'

'I shut yo' mout' for yo' by'n'by, yo' bloody stink-shit woman.' When she raised the crutch to him he yelled, 'Yo' look-out . . . I give you spear!'

'Yo' try it, blackfeller!'

'I don' try it time I do . . . I *do* it . . . properly, yo' bloody halfcaste rubbitch!'

He turned to Prindy: 'We got 'o go. Spone dat-one daid daddy belong 'o you, he mek him trouble long o' we. Come on. Gitchim swag, lil bits tucker. I wipe him out track.' Even spirits need tracks to find those they would haunt. There was no doubt about the fear of those two unbelievers in Blackfeller Bijnitch, the care they stepped with in clearing out. George told them to stay behind and take the consequences. They ignored him. He was compelled to erase their tracks along with his own by means of his magic brush. Anyway, Prindy, working with his own brush would have done it for them, would have had no choice in the matter, indeed, so close did they stick to him during the exodus; and surely he would have wanted to so it.

The incident happened in mid-morning. By noon they were clear of Mooragetaghee and heading southward through open forest. Beyond, the view from the mountain top had shown a strip of plain with a line of billabongs down the middle of it, running southward to infinity. They would be following the billabongs, George said. They would camp on a billabong tonight. He spoke of the billabong country, travelled by him in youth, as a veritable Eden. 'Full of ev'ryt'ng' he said, meaning that it was a land of super-abundance.

The forest thinned out to the plain, a silver sea of mirage in distance, at close hand grey cracked mud with a stubble of bleached grass regrown from the annual burning off of the rank stuff of Wet Season by hunting

Koongyarrakuns. There was no water yet. Some of the first holes were damp enough to grow moss; but most were just hard-baked clay sterilized by rooting pigs. George had nothing to say about the vanished Eden, only that they must keep their eyes open for pigs, not only for food, but because the big ones were dangerous in places like this where there was no cover. Pigs, he explained, were reincarnated Chinamen. Certainly there were pigs about, judging by the stinking messed up water they first came to.

The Sun was red in the roadmaker's dust before they reached water they could drink, in a long thin pool with a scattering of red lilies and a few pandanus fringing reedy banks—and pigs. Mungus went racing to investigate the grunting, disappeared into reeds, came *kai-kai-kai-ing* out with a huge ridged-backed sow slavering on his very tail. George hit the monster with a boomerang, that bounced off as if it had struck rock. But the sow got a fright, swung away, and became a ball of dust racing and raging, evidently heading for the next billabong. The next generation of reincarnated Chinamen came out of the rushes in search of their coward mother, little fat balls of grey mud, squeaking and grunting. George took a quick look to see if they had a father, then gave the signal to attack. They got the lot, seven. Then when they made camp on the other side of the billabong, they ate three in chunks grilled on the coals of a fire made of pandanus pipes. Afterwards they dug a hole and shoved the coals into it, covered them with pandanus leaves, tossed in the other suckers, covered them with more leaves, and then with dirt, and left them to cook through the night. A purple night, and windless, and soundless save for the distant call occasionally of passing plovers. They lay armed in readiness for the return of the sow; but she never came. Only Igulgul came, sneaking red-faced and badly lopsided up the dusty eastern sky round about midnight.

As they proceeded next day, the billabongs became larger and more like billabongs than pig-wallows, even though the pigs were there in increased proportion to what there was to hog—not direct proportion, because they could not get at all of it, which was why it was still there. Where there was water of any depth above an adult pig's head there were blazing masses of lilies through which the ducks and geese swam and over which red-crested lotus birds trotted—it being one of the blessings of nature that the pig, as well as not being able to fly, is a poor swimmer, else Terra Australis would long ago have been overrun by pigs, might even have come to be ruled by them. Several times the party were challenged for the intrusion on their own heritage, and kept clear. At one particularly still-fertile spot they found traces of their own kind; but with the camp these others had used well back as precaution against the arrogance of the new owners.

George said the blacks who had been there were Koonyarrakuns who had come out of the utterly wild western region, a dozen or so, men, women, and children, evidently bound for the road-builders' camps, hungry for tobacco and tea and sugar, and a drop of grog, as even they, the freest people in the land, were wont to become. Their trading stuff was the narrow loins of their girls. George claimed to recognize the tracks of a couple of the men, and Queeny those of one of the women, Queeny adding, 'Dat bloody lubra owe me money . . . promise gitchim what I been lend him from Chinaman. She gitchim all right, I know. But she been gamble all-lot, playin' card. I belt him dat-one.

They made camp that evening on the biggest billabong they had yet come to, where there were no pigs at all, but what was worse, the remains of several, piles of guts that were still being pulled about by kites and crows, and stinking to clean blue heaven. Also there were no water-birds, except half a dozen or so lying as little islands of bright blown-up feathers each with its cloud of bluebottles, out amongst the lilies where it was dangerous for anyone but a blackfellow to swim. That the despoilers weren't black was evident from the tracks of motor vehicles, scattered beer bottles, a couple broken, newspaper in sheets and scraps, some of the scraps lying with a couple of heaps of what looked like squirming heaps of irridescent metal, so thick were they with happy bluebottles, but were in fact what their owners would probably have called *coprus*—because, according to the knowledgeable Queeny, airing her knowledge in response to the

little-literate Prindy's puzzling over the odd lettering on other bits of the paper, they were Greeks. Evidently the spoliation was the result of a week-end's recreation by road-workers. Still George had nothing to say about the change in conditions since his youthful vision of the place as an Eden. His main concern was in looking about for cigarette butts, to augment the almost depleted tobacco supply of the party.

Next day there was further evidence that human beings of one of the oldest civilizations had taken over the region from the pigs in a way to make it seem that the pig is a cleanly animal. Still no comment from George, only a tinful of second-hand tobacco that reaked of garlic, beer, and pyorrhoea.

That evening saw them passing out of the domain of the pigs and those who were coming to be called, officially at any rate, New Australians,—to spare them the hurt of such names as Dago, Ox-cheek, Hun, Wop, Balt, Pom, commonly used by Old Australians (white),—and entering that of horned cattle and the superior Old Australians who herded them for their lordly Pommy Master, Alfred Vaisey. The last of the billabongs were fouled with cattle dung and churned up mud out of which bleached bones and horns protruded. But they were not troubled about water, because on the very edge of the plain a windmill was rising up to meet them.

A few head of stock bearing the Vaisey brand were drinking at the iron trough, Corellas like a pinking evening cloud hovering over the spinning mill as if waiting for it to stop to let them perch, as indeed some were already perched on the yawing vane. On the fence of a small wire stockyard a few kites were preening, to sit erect and watchful when the cockies gave the warning of approaching humanity. A couple of spur-wing plovers swept up shrilly calling from the earthen tank behind a netting fence into which the pumped water shot in silvery spurts. It looked as if the party were going to pass by. But it was a stratagem. Round the other side of the tank the men dropped down by the fence, sheltered by tall weeds growing inside, while the women went on towards a couple of biggish bloodwood trees, watched by the corellas. The kites, now in the air, saw the men, but gave no signal, evidently thinking it all that the corellas deserved to be sneaked on when they had eyes to see and wings to fly if not the sense to mistrust every human being.

George raked four cockies off the vane with a boomerang, and put another up into the mauve cloud that swept over them to protest against the treachery of it, bringing down another two. With that the remainder left, and the kites whistled to each other and dropped back to the stock-yard fence to await such pickings as would be. The women came to drink from the trough and fill the billy. Then camp was made under one of the trees; and the kites moved in to join the party. Prindy sang to all of them his song *Gilly Galah*, while the Sun went down and the mauve and crimson of the dead birds went up in smoke to join that of the sky.

They went on next morning into open forest. Everywhere now were signs of His Lordship's, the absent landlord's, stock: countless hoof-torn pads crisscrossing through the cropped clumps of rusty kangaroo grass and broken speargrass; new pads, little rivers of dust, old ones, scoured out by Wet Season rains, miniature gullies exposing the conglomerate beneath the skin of grey talc. No more knee-deep Flinder's grass growing on the little flats that wound between the hummocks of raised ground as when only the kangaroo as herbivore roamed the land. The little flats were bare white patches. Every shady spot was now a dung heap.

The calling of cattle was now the music of the land. They had to be careful when they came on cattle camped in shade, because if disturbed the beasts would rise, first gallop off in alarm, then in curiosity turn and follow, bawling to each other, spreading the disturbance, till the original disturbers had to bolt to shake them off—not out of fear of the beasts, but fear of those who attended them. It was a statutory offence to disturb stock. That meant it was also an offence for Aborigines to travel over stock-runs, even if the region might have been their tribal ground—not statutory, perhaps, but no less a law of the land, introduced with settlement and well and truly laid down with the rifle, the stockwhip, and the hobble-chain. It wasn't that the stockmen, even if they owned the stock, loved their beasts so well as to be distressed over upsetting of their natural placidity, but that disturbance caused them to become restless, to herd, which meant to fight and rut and consequently to lose weight; and weight in saleable beef is the measure of the butcher's interest in his victims.

That night they camped on the muddy water of a stream that George said was one of the heads of the Caroline River. White cockatoos warned every creature in screaming distance of their presence. Nevertheless, a young wallaby came to drink within easy spear throw. George left it to Prindy. 'Poor bugger,' said Prindy, breaking the struggling beast's neck with a boomerang. Whether or not bovine beasts, being as it were New Australians, responded like indigenous creatures to cockatoos' vigilance, a mob gathered round them in the night to moo softly and sigh and chew the cud, so many that in the morning they, the indigenous ones, had to slink away in various directions to begin with, to prevent the cavalcade that would have been on their heels. Caroline Station homestead was not

far away from here, according to George, who said that he spent a little time there after bringing cattle across from the Princess Alice for butchering for the gold miners. He said, 'Dat-lot whitefeller, Chinee . . . him proper mad long 'o dat-one goold. He been dig him, he been dig him . . . all day, all night, dig him . . . hot weather, cold weather, rain, no matter.'

'Wha' nam' goold?' asked Prindy.

'I don't know properly,' George confessed. 'Dey reckon for mek money. Dat time I young feller I ask old feller. . . .'

Queeny protested: 'Gwan, rubbitch! Mek him money from silber, ain't it? Dat-one goold for put him rotten tooth, mek him weddin' ring.'

'Wha' nam' weddin' ring?'

'You see on white lady hand . . . some halfcaste . . . and lubra, too. I been get one box from Chinaman before . . . sell him two bob. Woman got him weddin' ring, da's mean she marrit . . . all-same some silly bloody blackfeller mob cut him off finger, knock him out tooth.'

'Goold for mek money,' said George stubbornly.

Queeny yelled, 'Don' you listen bloody mungus blackfeller, boy. Where you see goold money?'

'Arrhhh!' was George's comment. Queeny was even crankier than usual, because the tobacco had petered out and she had not got anything like George's share in those findings.

What had been done to the country they had passed through, by pigs and cattle, was nothing compared with what the gold miners of forty or fifty years before had done to the region they now entered. It was hereabouts that Civilization of the land had begun in force where the process known as Opening Up The Country had really begun. Quite literally had this country been Opened up. Disembowelled would be an apter term. Not a creek but its banks had been stripped to the rock, the detritus and humus gathered over a millenium and more put through the cradle and the dry-blower, washed away, blown away, its rock split with dynamite, its trees torn down for building and for firewood, seeds and seedlings dead for ever for want of earth to root in—because there was gold in that earth, to be got at only by destruction of the earth. Not a quartz-topped hill, some obvious symbol of the wonders of the Dreamtime which originally must have flashed to Sun and Moon like jewelled giants, but had been blasted into heaps of graveyard gravel for the gold in their hearts. The heart-stuff had been taken and ground to powder under the stamps of batteries now lying collapsed in rusty iron tangles amidst harsh thickets of whiteman's and Chinaman's weeds, looking like the ground-down molars of old men's jaw-bones protruding from upheaved graves. That powder had been reduced to cyanided sludge to leach out the last pennyweight of the metal so precious that a country had been stolen for it, and that country heedlessly destroyed along with its owners. They had piped away the poison sludge to silt the creeks and rivers and kill all life that these supported, to spread sterility without effort into places not considered worth effecting it with pick and shovel and dynamite. There were no more grassy flats. All that grew out of the level land, besides the weeds, the stinking-rodger, the castor-oil bush, the Chinee burrs, were the slow-decaying parts of the edifices erected by those who had brought Civilization into the land, their homes for the period of spoliation, their places of trading for greedy exploitation of the fruits of greed, the rusting iron, broken brick, shattered glass, of the shops and pubs.

Amidst the wreckage of what George declared had been the township of Golden Grove, where there was a pool of muddy water behind a weir across a waste of sand that had been the Caroline River, George called a halt in mid-afternoon. There were a few paperbarks and river-gums growing in the sand, all but dead, hanging onto the earth by one root and the sky with one branch. Evidently George wanted to recapture something of the wonder he had experienced in what had been the first town he had seen. 'Crise,' he said. 'Goot time here den. Plenty people . . . whitefeller, blackfeller, Chineeman, Scottyman, Narishman, Germanman . . . any kind. Properly dat time. Ev'rybody drinkin', gamblin', playin'-up. By crise, yes . . . properly!' He sighed.

Evidently the fate of those of his breed who had been dispossessed of something they would have loved as only primitive man can love, his stamping ground, did not occur to him.

The water was bitter with the black concoction of macerated leaves and iron-rust. They drank it, made tea with it, camped in the sand under one of the mummified trees. No birds here to call the end of day. Even the *koodooks*, the vengeful Shades of tribesmen whose Dreaming Place has been destroyed since there was no calling of them in the night...*Koodook-koodook-koodook*...had abandoned it. There was scuffling round them in the early darkness, and tiny eyes to be seen like sparks. George said they were rats. Then in the middle of the night, as Igulgul was rising, they were wakened by a scream amongst the ruins across the way that had them up out of their sacking staring-Again: *Row-wow-wow—yee-yowl!*

'Pussy-cat,' said George.

The cats fought for all the rest of the night. The rats scuttled round the sand, trying to get at the bit of ripening wallaby hanging in the sugar-sacks from a bit of dead limb, only to be silently pounced on by Mungus. Igulgul was winking through the few leaves of the tree when Queeny woke them out of the bit of sleep they were at last enjoying, screaming again of the Black Flying Fox of Death: 'Le' me 'lone you black bastard!'

They left the ravaged country, to enter another shitty hoof-ripped tooth-torn stock-run, yellow earth and mean trees, a hint of inland, similar to Beatrice River country, on which fact Nell remarked with lively interest. George told Prindy that indeed they were getting near to the Beatrice, that tonight they would camp on the Princess Alice, from the head of which, where the railway crossed, it was only a good day's walk to Beatrice township. Prindy asked how far it was from here to the railway.

Distance is a relative thing, miles, the *mille passuum* of the Romans, the thousand paces, having as many meanings as modes of travelling them and moods of travellers. Primitive man's estimate is hard to beat: No-more long way, little-bits long way, lo—ng way, lo—ng way too much, for rough estimate—for accuracy reference to the passage of the Sun while one walks with purpose. George answered by turning his head to the brassy East, and fixing a point about thirty degrees from the zenith with his lips, swept them down to the horizon: hence two-thirds of a day's brisk walking, four hours, twelve miles.

They came to the Princess Alice River in mid-afternoon, in time for fishing for supper in a big hole where numerous cormorants showed the fishing must be good, a circumstance that caused annoyance to the women, who declared they wanted to go on to the railway. Queeny went so far as to start out for the railway, along the well-defined motor road they found following the river on the southern side—the road from Alice River Station, she and Nell declared, remembered from the old days; but she had to come back, because Nell would not go without Prindy, who ignored his mother as completely as George did. It was tobacco Queeny wanted. George, on the other hand, was not so hungry for the whiteman's weed as for a bit of fish he called Parunga, best of all fish, he declared, to be found only in the Alice and Queen Victoria Rivers, and always in holes like this. Queeny's assertion that the parunga was *Wahji* probably made Prindy all the more interested. George countered that by saying the fish was *Wahji* only when caught by women and boys, but not so if an initiated man gave it to them. The women cast themselves down in the shade of a big leaning paperbark to watch.

Catching the parunga required special technique besides the Singing of him. The great fish had a special weakness, an appetite for cormorants, the scourge of all other fish. Occasionally he would get one in a dive. What they needed was a cormorant. The fishing flock of about a dozen had moved upstream a bit at the arrival of the party, to sit in a line on the branch of a big submerged tree, watching. George got Prindy to walk slowly towards them along the water's edge, pretending to fish with his spear, while he himself, under cover of another tumbled tree trunk, went up the bank and worked his way along until he was just beyond them. He aimed his boomerang. The birds started at sound of its whistling rush, turned—too late. Two went down. Prindy came running to retrieve them. One disappeared as he was swimming out. He got the other. George told him to climb onto the tree and wait for him. George came out with spears and his sugar-sack. He took hibiscus string from the bag and tied it to the dead bird, tossed it into the water. He was certain that the other had been taken by a parunga and that all they had to do was to wait. They waited so long that Queeny and Nell collected witchetty grubs they found in large quantity in rotten flood timber and pencil yams, and having got a fire going to cook them, called Prindy to come and eat. Prindy ignored them.

It was sundown, with the hole becoming a lake of blood white-spotted with the reflexions of all the cockatoos in the country gathering in the trees to mock, and Queeny joining in with peals of nasty laughter—when there was a flurry in the green darkness down below, and spearman and henchman grew rigid again as countless times they had for flickering instants, but now held their poses—a great toothy cave of a mouth rising to snap—*tuk*! George's barbed spear shot past the floating bird. The mouth clamped over the spear. Spear vanished. George looked at Prindy with a grin: 'He come up by'n'by.' He looked up at the cockies, round at the women. All were silent. A blue crane high in a tree croaked whatever his opinion was, and then went flapping off, perhaps to spread the story of it.

The cockatoos yelled again when they saw the haft of the spear appear down by the bar, wag feebly. George said quick, they must get him, before he drowned and sank. The water was quite shallow where they got him, gasping his life out with his blood. He was a type of cod, a good three feet in length, and of such a weight as to need the pair to carry him and cause the heavy spear to bend. The cockatoos raised a great shout about it. The women only stared.

The fishermen cut great fillets from it and grilled them. Prindy offered the first piece to his mother, but to have her refuse it, saying shrilly, 'Dat no-goot tucker.' Prindy said his uncle had said he could give it to her, and that would make it right. She persisted, 'I don' wan' . . . and you leave him 'lone too . . . poison dat one . . . mek you blow up and get him sore all over. Don' you eat him . . . don' you, now!' But Prindy gobbled the fillets with his uncle, remarking over and over on its tastiness. The rest went into a ground oven, to taunt the hungry women all night with its sweet savour

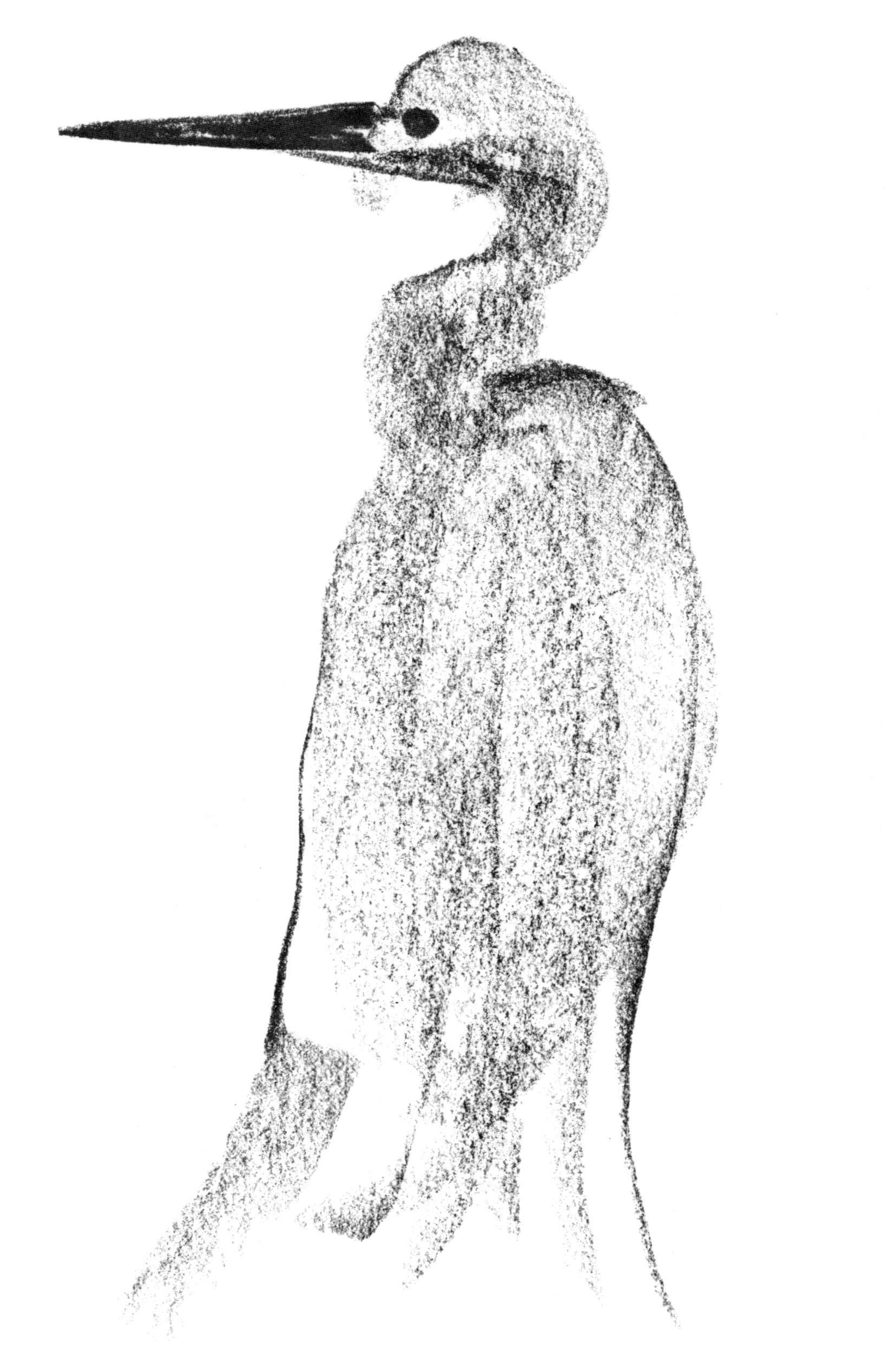

hanging over the camp like a haunting ghost.

Queeny, usually the last to rise, was first up next morning, bustling in the half-light to get her things together. Nell was up a little later, roused by the movement, likewise Prindy, to whom she said shortly, 'Come on . . . we go now.' She grabbed his arm, pulled when he would have turned to George, who still appeared to be asleep. Mungus came leaping into it, *kai-kai-kai-ing* in disapproval of trouble he suspected between his people. George grunted out of his sacking, 'You go, *Kookanjinni*.' Prindy looked surprised, bewildered. Without a word he took up his belongings. Queeny was already up on the road, calling, rousing the sleepy cockatoos.

It was luxurious going, following a silky pad after making your own road through the wilderness. How long since a motor vehicle had passed would be impossible to say, because cattle also used the twin tracks in what would be daily movements to and from water. The road pretty nearly followed the river, as would be necessary in the old days when waggon horses needed watering. Obviously there were short-cuts across the bends. But that would mean picking their way again. No need to hide their tracks, when invisible stock, already calling themselves together for the daily plod, would soon obliterate them. So easy was it that by mid-morning, Prindy, in the lead with Mungus, declared that he could hear motor car ahead, the sound not coming towards them but crosswise to their going. Then the others heard it—droning, constant, waxing and waning on the wind. Then suddening—*poom*! It was a good way off. Still the air quivered to it, the leaves of the trees whispered, birds called alarm. It happened again, twice. The dust could be seen rising. Prindy explained to the women.

It was Mungus, out in front, who picked up the tracks first—a single pair of human footprints. Eventually he knew whose they were, by his quivering interest. Prindy also recognized them at once. As the others came up, looking anxious, he said, 'Ngangul.'

Queeny exclaimed, 'How dat bloody old bastard get 'head o' we?'

Prindy said, quite seriously, 'Might-be he fly.'

'Don' be jitty,' snapped Queeny. 'Man can't fly!'

'You been tell him 'bout hangel.'

'Dat-one hangel long o' 'Eaven . . . no-more dis country. He daid feller.'

Prindy said, 'Dat-one Pookarakka can fly.'

His mother said shrilly, 'Rubbitch . . . dat old man he on'y gammon . . . bloody rogue. You finish long o' dat-lot now.'

Prindy turned away with a silent *Brrrp* of the lips, went on in old Njorgunga's tracks.

Mungus smelt George before they were anywhere near him, or perhaps more truly his cooking, because for a little while he trod warily, sniff-sniff-sniffing the breeze. Prindy with spear poised watched as warily. Then Mungus gave a yelp and dashed ahead and would not stop on the hissed order. Prindy ran after him while his mother cried in subdued voice for him to come back.

There was George sitting amongst dried cow-dung in the shade of a *mangun* plum, with a good coal fire, the billy boiling, and chunks of baked fish laid out on bushes. 'Goot-tay,' he said casually as Prindy came running up. 'You want him breakfas'?'

He had no weapons or dunnage of any kind with him. When he saw Prindy looking about, he said, 'Been plant him.'

As the women came up, Queeny demanded, 'Wha's matter you foller-in' up we, old man? We finish long o' you.'

Nevertheless they all ate, while butcher birds gathered for the scraps.

They set off again, with George leading, not bothering to take short-cuts, as he must have on his own. Their progress towards civilization was soon to be measured not only by the waxing sound of it, the roar and rumble, but by the smell, the dust, the smoke of gasoline and dieseline and gelignite. Then they could see it, as a red haze hanging over hills to southward, whither the road was turning them. Now there was dust to be seen dulling the natural sheen of leaves evolved to reflect a blasting Sun and now tending to wither under it—dust, dust, dust—on everything. The guts of animals that ate the grass must be full of mud. It stung the eyes—or was it the fuming exhalations of the *kuttabah's* mechanical monsters?

The country was becoming rocky, the banks of the river high, the stream more rapid in its little flow. Signs of civilization in the form of tree-stumps, rusty cans, bottles, spent cartridges. Then suddenly there it was across the river, a very different place from that Nell and Prindy had looked out upon from the train half a year earlier—the couple of railway cottages, the shed in which their porcine progenitor lay dying. Now along the river bank stretched a township of tents, tin sheds, bush houses, laid out in orderly fashion, as it were in streets. As the timber on that side had been mostly felled, but was still thick on their side and thicker for regrowth from the stumps, the party were able to see without being seen, especially as the place was almost deserted and its few inhabitants preoccupied. Three or four people wearing white aprons, one a woman, were to be seen moving rapidly between a big tin building that was obviously the kitchen and a bigger one of bush materials that by the long table and line of bottled condiments and covered dishes was seen to be the mess room. Several dogs were sitting watching at respectful distances, and kites and crows from the few remaining trees.

Queeny said, 'Wha' you-call-yim Renchouse, eh? Dat woman white.'

The woman was really red, face and fat arms, as she moved back and forth through the slit of blazing sunshine between the two buildings.

Nell said, 'Close-up dinner-time, I reckon.'

Almost as she said it, the rolling mechanical roar that came like the sound of surf on a shore, waxing, waning, stopped dead. They turned towards the silence. A few minutes of nothing but the surge of the south-easter in the trees. Then mechanical sound again, the steady drone of an ordinary motor vehicle. There was increased bustle in the Renchouse. Soon there was the roaring of a truck going into low gear, its whining down a declivity, its howling up another. Out of the screen of spared trees a big red truck came rolling, its tray packed with yellow men, trailing a cloud of yellow dust that the wind swept across the river to smother more leaves. The truck drew up at another long bush shelter. The men leapt out of it, beating the dust from their clothes, went into shelter, to wash at a trough.

Another truck, of indeterminate colour but with a similar load of men, rolled in behind. Soon a mob of red men were at the table, wolfing like starvelings, so that the clatter of their dealings with their provender was to be heard by the watchers, even though they were somewhat up-wind of them. Prindy declared that they were eating roast beef and puddin'. None of the party appeared to envy the men their provender. It was when the meal was done and the mob sat back and filled the mess room with blue smoke that there was swallowing and sighing. Half the men retired to their tents.

Then movement again. The trucks sounded their horns. The red men gathered slowly. All aboard. Then off again; and only the drone of their going; and at length again the roaring of their machine-monsters gouging the way to progress.

Dogs and birds in the camp came hurtling to squabble over the buckets of scraps being dumped in a hole behind the kitchen. More empty cans and bottles came rolling down the river bank. The kitchen people dispersed to separate tents. George said he would go see if he could get tobacco. When Queeny took money from her drawers and offered it he ignored her.

George was in no hurry. First he explored the river bank further up, then came back to cross by a shallow stretch, to saunter into the camp. The dogs bailed him up, until someone's head appeared at the fly of a tent. With the dogs called off, he went to speak with the head. After some minutes, he went on to another tent, remote from the rest, closest to the kitchen and beside a tin shed. Here he stopped for some time, evidently talking with someone inside who eventually passed him out a tin of tobacco. Rolling a cigarette, he then went to the woodheap, and after some luxurious puffing and surrounded by the dogs, he took up an axe and began, in leisurely style, to split skillets off sawn blocks. He was on the job long enough to take three spells and smoke three cigarettes, to the annoyance of Queeny, who kept saying, 'Bloody black bastard. . . mekin' me-feller do perish!' Prindy offered to go over and get a pinch for them, but to be quickly told *no-more*! What if George had taken a job there, intending to stay on? Then, the women said, they would clear out tonight and head down the railway. But Queeny

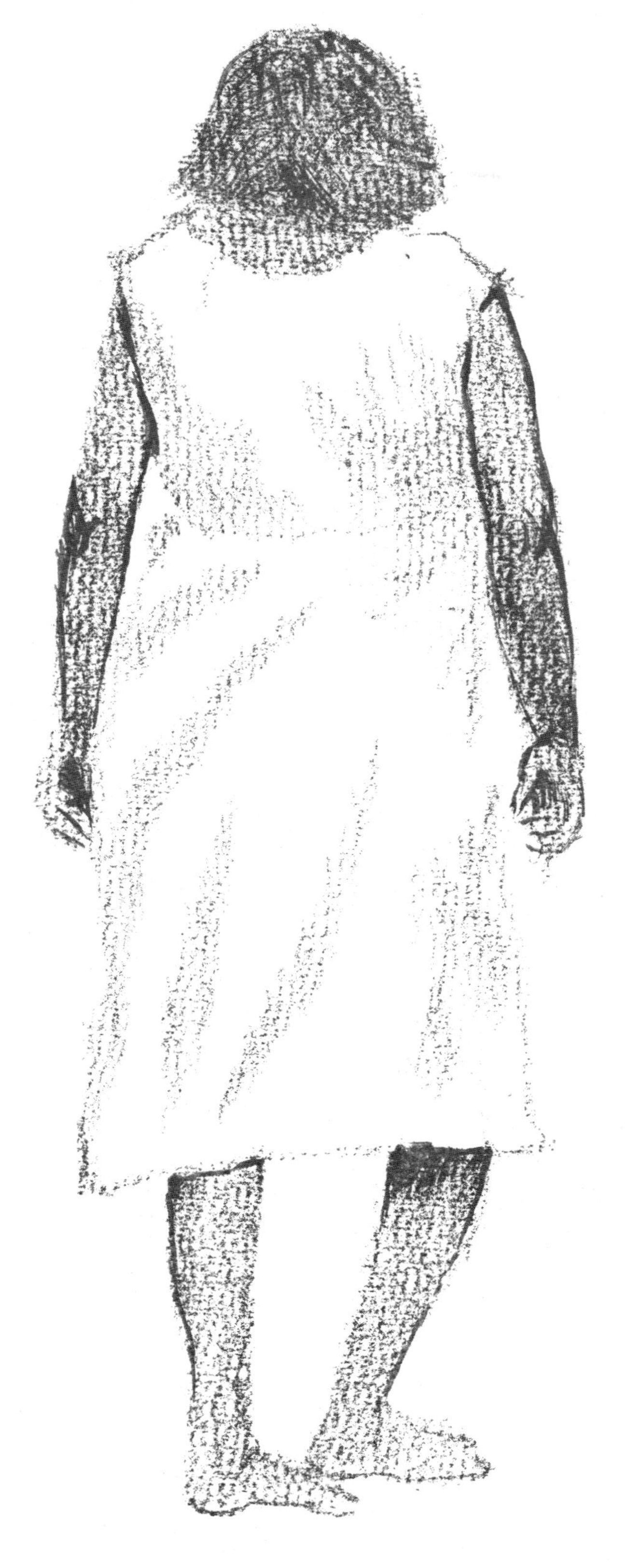

sighed and moaned, 'By crise, I like him smoke too-much!' As if to taunt them, George kept a haze of smoke about him.

The Sun was halfway down the sky, when out of that end tent came a bulky red man wearing white singlet and khaki pants. The first thing he did was to scan the opposite bank as looking for something there, evidently through having been told about the presence of the others, which caused them to withdraw further into cover, muttering, 'Wha's matter him tell-him-'bout we?' He didn't see them. Then he went to the shed next door and opened it, and after a while reappeared carrying a sugar-sack containing something. From there he went to the kitchen, to be seen again heading for the woodheap with a sack now looking quite bulky. He gave the sack to George, who set down the axe and turned with him in another glance across the way. Then waving farewell, they parted, the man to go back to the kitchen, George to come strolling out of the camp. But instead of heading back to those awaiting him, George went the very opposite way, over the road and up the slight incline to the railway siding. He stopped at the water-tank to drink from a tap, then stood for a while in the shade, looking about, but never across the river. Queeny boiled over with annoyance: 'Dat bloody bastard all-day he been mek him sumpin trouble! I glad time I finish long o' him for bloody puggin goot.'

Behind the siding was a wall of rock, hacked out of the hill that there sloped south-westward, diverting the river sharply. The railways vanished into cuttings on either side. George set off down the railway southward, sack on his back, disappeared into that cutting. 'Where he go now?' moaned Queeny.

Now the road-camp was astir again, with those people beginning to bustle about the Renchouse. The party divided its attention between them and looking for George. First indication of George was a squeak from Mungus, who was promptly slapped by Queeny. Mungus had smelt him. Then Prindy heard him. Soon he was seen coming through the timber on their side of the river. George said they would go down the river a bit and back from it, so as to light a fire and eat. When they were settled down, he brought some of the stuff out of the bag: bread and beef and tea and sugar, tobacco, matches, cigarette papers. Queeny settled back in deep content to smoke while the billy boiled.

As they ate, George related through Prindy what, ostensibly, had passed between him and the big red man, who it seemed was the Boss of the Renchouse. Today was Friday. Tonight most of the road workers would be leaving camp, to spend the week-end at either the Beatrice or the Caroline townships. The red man himself would be going to Beatrice, but later than the others, because he had to see to the cleaning up after their meal and other things. George had asked him for a lift, explaining that he had a couple of wives, one a young halfcaste, whom he didn't want the mob of whitemen to see, because he'd heard they were a no-goot lot; not that he minded one goot whiteman having her. So the man had said, all right, bring her down tonight, and he would take them all down the line and drop them off where they liked.

Nell snapped at him, 'You been sell him me like lubra!'

George said to Prindy, 'Wha' two-feller you Mumma, Aunty, goin' 'o do? Dat long way yet long o' Beatrice. Plenty road-camp. Plenty motor car come. P'liceman, too. Dat man been talk p'liceman been come look-about you. One young colour boy, got him halfcaste mumma, he reckon. . . .'

Nell gasped, 'You been tell him dat man 'bout my boy?'

George said patiently, still addressing Prindy, 'Nutching I been tell him dat man. . . on'y 'bout woman wan' lift. Spone dat two-feller go long o' man tonight, get in truck, you 'n-me two-feller meet him dere long o' crossing. You stop behind lil bits. He can't see you motor car light. All right, when he stop for pick me hup, you come out, jump up in truck behind. Man can't see you. I black him you face. . . Here!' He took up a lump of charcoal, crushed it in his fist, and as Prindy, grinning, thrust his face to him, daubed his cheek. Prindy chuckled. His mother scowled. Queeny was expressionless.

Just then their attention was diverted by a sound coming from northward, from amongst the hills. Prindy quickly identified it, 'Motor trolley belong to railwayman.' Soon, with engine popping and wheels howling, a section trolley burst from the cutting, to go right by. Prindy cried, 'Mist' Toohey!' It was, indeed, Tom Toohey, riding with one of his gang. They vanished into the southern cutting, in a moment were heard clanging over the little railway bridge, then lost in the din of the road machines. Nell said with a sigh that Tom Toohey was a goot man, with a coloured family, who would have given them a lift and not betrayed them.

'No matter,' said Queeny. 'We go long o' dis man, eh?'

Again Nell sighed.

Then that sudden silence fell again to southward. And soon the influx of the dusty men began, not merely two truckloads this time, but seven or eight, or nine or ten, it was impossible to see through their dust. Now there was a clamour of voices and banging of cans. The yellow men were darting about, lining up at a long shed where showers were streaming, and emerging from it as red-and-white men with towels about their waists.

The Sun went down. The sky behind the watchers blazed red, while that before them turned mauve against which the hills reared violet. Acetylene lights began to prick the gathering gloom. Some of the tents glowed with the light of lanterns. Then an iron clangour called the mob to mess; and they came like scurrying ants, khaki, white, blue.

After the meal the lights of trucks and cars blazed in the gathering gloom. The vehicles roared into life, went off with men in back and front, southward, northward. By the time it was fully dark, two-thirds of the men were gone and all but a couple of the motor vehicles. Obviously the others were remaining, sitting lounging at the mess table, or retired to lighted tents.

The light went out in the kitchen. Light came on in the Boss's tent. The silence that had hung for a long while over the watching party was broken by George's saying to Prindy, 'Come on...I mek him properly blackfeller you...den we go long o' crossing.'

The pale glow of Prindy's face and hair disappeared under charcoal, while the women watched. Then, taking up their belongings, the two set out the way George had come from up river.

Queeny called, 'Wha' 'bout dog?'

George answered without looking back, 'You tek him...put him truck.'

Mungus raised his voice in a thin howl as the males disappeared. '*Kaiatulli!*' snapped Queeny, and slapped him. He fell to sobbing softly to himself. 'We go, eh?' said Queeny, and heaved herself up, untied Mungus, but held the leash, took up her own sack of belongings. Sighing heavily, Nell also rose.

They went down and across by the way George had gone in the afternoon, but instead of heading straight for the Boss's tent, skirted the camp by going almost to the railway. Thus they got upwindward of the dogs, which came to them roaring. Mungus yapped in terror. Someone in the camp yelled, 'Shut up yo' bloody mongrels...lie down, there!' The dogs fell silent, let the intruders pass.

They came round by the wash-house and the stinking dunnies, struck back to the place they sought, came slowly up to it. For a moment they stood staring at the glowing canvas. Then Queeny coughed. A deep voice growled inside, 'Who's 'at?'

Queeny gave Nell a little shove. Approaching the fly, Nell said softly, 'Boss.'

Sound of creaking canvas and bare feet slapped on the ground, and the voice: 'Yeah...what is it?'

Nell hesitated: 'We...we come, Boss.'

A deep inhalation: 'All right...come on in.'

Slowly Nell lifted the fly, to behold the red man, redder than ever at close quarters and by contrast with his white sleeveless singlet, a fleshy biggish man, seated on the edge of a high camp-stretcher, the round face tight with cautious expectancy. The wide slit of mouth opened, revealing teeth in a grin: 'Ullo!'

Nell replied with a breath. The man said, 'Well, come on in...don' be shy.'

As Nell came in, she looked back at Queeny. The man asked, 'Who's out there?'

'My tchister.'

'Well, tell her to piss off . . . I don' wan' two yo'.' When Nell hesitated, he raised his voice slightly: 'Go on, you out there. Your sister'll be all right. You go back your old man.' Then to Nell, as he rose, 'Come 'n' sit down . . . we'll 'ave a drink . . . whisky.'

There was only the bed to sit on. The one chair was cluttered with smoking gear and an alarm clock. For the rest the place was packed with boxes, cartons, suitcases. A pressure lantern hung from the ridge pole. He took a bottle and glasses from one of a stack of kerosene cases serving as a cupboard. 'Sit down', he said again. She sat gingerly on the edge of the bed. He filled a glass, handed it to her, saying, 'Good lookin' girl, all right. Wha's yo' name?'

She breathed, 'Nelly,' taking the glass.

He filled his own glass, set the bottle on the chair, sat beside her. 'Here's fun,' he said, taking a swig. She took a sip. 'Come on, drink up!' She took another sip.

'Where d' you come from, Nelly?'

'Bush.'

'Wha's a pretty girl like you doin' livin' out 'n the bush . . . and with 'n old bloke like that? Come on . . . drink it up!' He swigged his off.

She muttered, 'Too sitrong.'

'Drop o' water, eh?' He reached for a water-bag also hanging from the ridge-pole. ''Alf an' 'alf, eh?' He filled his own, swigged heavily. Looking at her worn and rumbled dress he said, Need new dress. I got some there. Take that one off.' He leapt up again, to open a suitcase and rummage, and bring out several print dresses. 'Try 'em for size . . . and style, eh?' He chuckled. 'Take that one off, anyway.'

She muttered, 'No-more.'

'Gawn . . . don' be silly. S'pose yo' run naked roun' the bush. What yo' gettin' coy for now? Drink that up and then see what dress you wan'.'

'I don' wan' him dress, Boss.'

'Well, wha' yo' wan'...money?'

'On'y wan' go long o' Beatrice.'

'Eh?'

'You tek him me Beatrice, eh?'

'I'll take you some time...Races...but they ain't for long while yet ...couple o' months.'

'I wan' 'o go tonight, Boss?'

'Eh?'

'You been promised old-man, ain't it?'

'I never promised him nothin'. I give him a swag o' tucker and tobacco for a lend o' you.'

She stared at him.

'What's wrong't you?' he asked irritably. 'Come on...get your dress off....'

'No-more, Boss!'

As she made to rise, he pushed her down again: 'No, you don',' he snapped. 'I paid for it...I get it.'

'You tek me Beatrice....'

'I'll take you bloody nowhere...'ere!' He grabbed her. Then his voice changed, to wheedling, 'Come on, be sensible girl. Take off yo' clothes. I look out for you. I give you job in kitchen. Your old man can work on the wood 'eap ... come on, come on!' He dragged up her skirt. She had nothing under it. 'Oh!' he cried, and chuckled, and pulling the dress up about her waist, pushed her back on the bed. 'Oh!'

'No-more, no-more....'

He was panting now, holding her down by a red hand on her chest, while, goggling at her, he tore open his fly.

'You tek me....'

Her voice was smothered by the weight of him, his walloping about on top of her, so that the timber of the stretcher cracked.

Then he lay panting: 'Jesus...Jesus Christ!' He was slobbering. Now he giggled, 'Tha's good...eh, tha's bes' poke I ever 'ad. You goin' 'o be my girl, eh? My girl. I look after you good.' He heaved up from her, panting, quivering, reached for the tobacco. She sat up, pulling down her dress.

'Don' cover it up,' he said, licking a cigarette. He gave her the cigarette, lit it, turned to make one for himself, chuckling all the while. 'You work for me, eh? I look out for you good. You sleep with me tonight, eh?'

She said desperately, 'I wan' 'o go Beatrice, Boss.

'Not tonight, sweetheart. 'Ere, 'ave some more grog.'

'Tomorro' you tek me?'

'No, I can't take you yet. I got to stay 'ere.'

'Old-man been say. . . .'

'If he said I was takin' you, he's a bloody liar. He asked me if I was goin' . . . and I said, No. I said I can't leave this place with all these thievin' bastards 'ere. I give him all that stuff for lend of you for the night. He said okay. Now, take off that dirty rag of a thing and I'll give you a new dress . . . and we'll 'ave a bit of a party, and then another naughty, eh? Yaahhhhh!'

She leapt up, eyes wide, mouth open. 'Eh . . . wha's matter?' he asked.

'I got 'o go,' she panted.

'No you don'!' He made a grab at her. But she jerked out of his grip, burst out of the tent.

The dim figure of Queeny could be seen sitting on a box near by. Nell rushed at her: 'Dat old man . . . he talk liar,' she said urgently 'Come on!'

'Wha' nam'?' hissed Queeny.

The Boss was at his tent-fly, peering out. In a lowered voice he called, 'Wha's goin' on?'

Nell seemed not to notice him, dragged Queeny to her feet: 'Dat old-man been steal him my boy.'

Queeny cried, 'Eh, look out! Then, as she swung along after Nell, with Mungus pulling at his lead, she asked, 'Wha' for you talk like o' dat? Old-man say meet him long o' road.'

'Him talk liar . . . dat man been tell him me. I been all-day fright' dat bloody bastard goin' 'o tek my boy sometime . . . I been tell him you . . . I

been tell him you . . . Now he gone!'

'Wha' you goin' 'o do, Tchister?'

'I got 'o run-him-up.'

'You can't gitchim dat-lot.'

'I gitchim all right. Where dat dog. Here, dog, you foller-him-up!'

Mungus gave a yap as if he understood, and straining on the leash, and with the other dogs roaring in the rear, took them back to the point where they had come from, then up along that bank of the creek where his other friends had gone. Easy going for a couple of hundred yards. Then they had to go down to the stream through a tumble of rocks where it swung towards road and railway, the foot of the hill across the way. It was slow going because of Queeny's disabilities and the deep darkness in there. They might as well have saved themselves the trouble, because that was the end of the trail as far as poor Mungus's faculties were concerned. It was lost in the water. He ran up and down either side of the star-streaked fluid blacker blackness that chuckled over and around the rocks, squeaking apologies for his limitations as more and more fiercely charged with them. Going on up further brought them to the concrete causeway on which the road, coming down through a cutting, crossed. Here things livened up for a minute or two when, a few yards up in the mud on the camp side Mungus found evidence that took him through another tumble of rocks to the railway. But evidently that was the way George had come during his leisurely walkabout of the afternoon. Mungus seemed to know it, and dragged Nell, the only one who could get through those rocks with him, back to the road crossing. They tried going up the other side, along the bank on top to right and left of the road. They came back and tried the rocky banks of the biggish pool spanned by the railway bridge. Mungus gave up with a dingo howl, in which Nell joined him: 'Oh, ow . . . where my lil boy . . . where you go, boy . . . where, where, where?' The camp dogs, not so far from the crossing, raised an echoing clamour.

All the while Queeny had been saying that George would have headed for the Alice River Country, that is the region further West where, joined by the Beatrice, the Alice truly became a river, the old man's own country. She said it again now, 'He been go Alice, all right. No goot look-about here. We can't find him track. He too goot, dat bloody black bastard. Two-feller got him dat-one brush, too. . . hide him tracks.'

Nell said promptly, 'We go Alice.'

'Eh, look out! Dat too much long way.'

'No-more long way. I been come dat road plen'y time, when I live long o' Mitchis Coon-Coon.'

'You ride long o' motor car dat time.'

'No matter. . . dat no-more long way.'

'Wha' you goin' do dere?'

'I tek him back my boy.'

'Might-be you can't find him dere.'

'I find him all right. I ask him dat station boss helip him me.'

'Might-be he tell him p'liceman.'

'I tchileep long him spone he want. . . I know dat man, Mist' Bolder.'

'Wha' 'bout ask him dat man dere tek we long o' motor car?' Queeny nodded towards the camp.

'He been say he can't go 'way from here.'

'Might-be tomorro' 'nother-one man.'

'No-more. I wan' 'o go now, Tchister. Come on, we go.'

Queeny protested, 'Too dark!'

'We can see dat road all right. Please you come, Tchister. I wan' my lil boy back. I don' wan' dat bloody black bastard breakin' him in. I tell him you before, I been dream dat-lot kill him my boy. 'Cause he not blackfeller dey wan' 'o kill him. Like dere behin' Catfish. I know dey goin' 'o kill my lil boy. You come now, please, Tchister.'

Queeny sighed heavily, then cried in sudden anger. 'All right, I come. Dis time I gitchim dat bloody black bastard I kill him daid. . . I get rifle from station. . . I buy him. . . I kill him daid, daid, daid!'

As they crossed the river again at that point lower down where they had gone to and from the road camp, the dogs started in on them again,

roaring along the bank. The beam of a flashlight swept along the trees above. Then—*bang*!—*wheeee*! A bullet went screaming over them. The rocky river-bed rang to the explosion. The dogs were silent. The pair stopped in their tracks. Then a great voice rose up from the camp, 'Go easy with that rifle, you silly bastard!'

Another voice answered, 'Pull your 'ead in, mug.'

'I'll punch your bloody 'ead in!'

'Come an' try it!'

Uproar of voices of men and the dogs again.

Nell and Queeny and Mungus went scrambling up the bank, crossed the road and straight into the bush. They stopped again. The voices were still raised, but distant now. After a moment they swung to the right in the direction of the road, gained it, and went swinging away along it, with *Minaiji*, the Evening Star, palely lighting their way.

By the same dim light, across a pale-earthed plain grown only with stunted bushes and lank broken grass, parallel to the Alice road and about a mile to South of it, George and Prindy, heel to toe, were heading in the same direction. Somewhere away to southward of them dingoes were howling in doleful chorus.

But for those following the road was not the easy way it had been by day, because used now by stock for bedding down, the beasts leaping up in fright before the yapping onslaughts of a diminutive debil-debil and the appearance of two grey ghosts, one with three legs, they were too astonished to move and had to be walked round. Queeny was scared of bulls, a couple of which were heard grumbling challenges. She told tales of acquaintances who had been chased by bulls. Nell kept on grimly, speaking only when Queeny complained of weariness, repeating shortly what she had said at first, that if they kept going, they might find those they sought camped where they had all camped last night. Queeny sighed and swung along, singing bits of hymns: 'Yas, Jesus luff me, yas, Jesus luff me, yas, Jesus luff me. . . de Bible tell me so. . . .'

After about two hours of it, with Minaiji down in the tree-tops, they came to a creek, one of many they'd had to cross, but this one with water winking at them. They stopped to drink. But Queeny said she couldn't go on without a drink of tea and a bite to eat. Nell agreed. They made a fire, boiled the billy, ate bread and beef with the tea. Meantime the star had gone, leaving a black black world behind, for all the blaze of other stars. Queeny said she was too done up to go on. Nell coaxed, screeched a bit, wept. But Queeny wouldn't budge. 'Stop worrit,' she said wearily. 'We gitchim all right. But no goot long o' dark.' Soon she was asleep. For a long while Nell whimpered crouched in the tiny glow of the fire, then sighing lay down in the cow-dung and slept.

Thus, while only a mile or so away up the same creek by another waterhole beside another tiny fire the quarry were sleeping. Dingoes were still howling away to southward.

Igulgul came up, winking through the trees, a skinny old fellow now, peeping, it seemed, at both parties, so near to each other and yet so remote. The dingoes got in between the two parties and howled to tell them of their proximity, so that they stirred in their sleep. Mungus woke, but made himself very small so as not to be seen or smelt. Evidently he didn't understand the lingo. Just before dawn the dingoes curled up in the way of their kind and fell asleep.

Both parties were up in moonlit lilac-tinted dawn, taking a hasty meal of the last of their bread, a swig of tea, then away. The Sun rose red behind them, turned to brass. The south-easter rose and lashed them on the flanks. The flies came to ride with them and drink their sweat.

In a couple of hours the women reached the point of long yesterday's beginnings. No sign there even of their own tracks now. Even the place where they had camped under the paper-bark was trodden over by cattle and torn about by birds after scraps. They paused only to drink. They went on till noon, when they came to a large stock yard that evidently had been worked only a day or two before. A couple of dead beasts, sick or maimed creatures that had been shot, lay behind the yard, attended by a large flock of kites and crows. Scraps of car tracks were to be seen amongst the hoofprints, and horse-prints amongst the bovine. There was a shed by the river, in which hung a food-safe from an ant-proofed hook. Inside they found a heel of stale bread and a small can of treacle. They had bread and treacle for dinner.

Southward, now some five miles distant, the others were making their way over grey plain grown with stunted bushes and lank grass. Good *beinook* country. Everywhere grey heads of bustards popped up to stare. George said they would wait till they came to water before they took one. They saw the waterhole a long way off, by reason of the small birds clouding over it. Only a couple of small trees, the only trees in miles. George said they would get a *beinook* now. He had Prindy break a bough off a bush and, raising it high, go walking ahead with it. The silly birds began to follow the odd thing, the walking tree, forgetful of the man walking with spear poised in womera. Prindy stopped, to wag the bush slowly. The *beinooks* approached it warily. *Zip*! The spear flew. Great grey wings outspread. A croaking of protest against the treachery. The stricken bird ran with the rest, but could not take the air, fell, to be pounced on by Prindy and despatched with a boomerang, and the usual apology, 'Poor bugger.'

The water in the hole was white as milk with clay, but cool and sweet. They drank deeply. Then they grilled their bird and ate great chunks of it, and afterwards slept for a little in a bit of shade; while a couple of kites circled waiting for them to be gone. They went on, taking half of the bustard with them.

The southern plain ran almost to the Alice River, so that it was not impossible that those kites in their highest orbit would have been able to see both parties. At any rate, there was a windmill by the river that the women saw rise up out of the river timber; while the men saw it as what looked like a taller tree in the wall of trees away away to their right.

The women came up to the windmill right glad of the water in the trough they had to share with a small mob of cattle, because hereabout the bed of the river was sandy and its flowing underground. They reached it with the gilding of the sky, just ahead of galahs homing after a day of foraging along the river. They brought down one each with sticks, and had them, little bags of bones, for supper. Then they got through the fence of the earthen tank and lay down to sleep in the weeds.

Those across the plain kept going longer, drawn by a force much more powerful than a couple of hours' thirst and the prospect of laying weary limbs down, for all its remoteness. George had been looking for it since noon. The haze of the dusty windy day had hidden it until the western sky reddened and revealed it as a small blue speck. George, who had been singing softly to himself, suddenly cried, '*Ngah gunga . . . ngah gunga* . . . my country, my country!' He explained that the speck was a peak in the sandstone country, called Aldinbinya, The Head. They would be going there, into the very heart of Aldinbinya, into its Snake Caves. 'Properly Tchineke country . . . properly belong Old Tchamala.'

The last of the red light revealed a blue wall of plateau, made by Tchamala, in his burrowings that had resulted in the river system of the country, Beatrice Alice, Queen Victoria, so George said. He sang of his country:

Gubbalinga, gubbalinga, ngah gunga
Gubbalinga, ngah, ngah.

They were just about to camp, when away somewhere to the south-east Prindy said he could hear plovers. That meant water. They headed that way, by the light of Minaiji—and sure enough, there was a *gilgai*, a little clay-hole shaded by bushes. While the plovers ran round them, scolding, mimicked by Prindy they made camp for the night.

In the clear morning air, The Head stood out more distinctly. George viewed it with face quivering. 'Long time I no see my country,' he said.

'*Gubbalinga, ngah gunga . . . ngah, ngah, ngah*!' As they went on their way westward he told of the wonderland it was, as so often during the long journey to it, but never with tears in eyes and voice as now. He pointed out where Alice River Station homestead lay, actually on the Beatrice River, just above the junction of the two streams. Nothing was to be seen there but the dark line of far off timber. He said they should reach the homestead by noon.

The other party, in trying to assess their own proximity to the homestead, made use of the windmill, up the twenty-foot ladder of which Nell went, to the great wonder and excitement of Mungus, to view the scene. She came down to report, 'Nutching . . . on'y tree, tree, tree.'

After a drink of tea strongly laced with treacle, they got on their way. Now the country was changing again from grey to yellow, the stunted beefwoods and mulgas that had lain between them and the plain that so narrowly kept them from what they were so widely seeking, giving way to open forest.

George now walked with sprightly step, telling Prindy how soon they would be entering upon their proper relationship of *Nungala* and *Wallanjinni*. Prindy must prepare himself for the ordeal of silence ahead of him for many a moon. The old men George would gather at the station would start the proceedings. One who stood in the relationship of father would give George formal permission to take charge of his nephew, one who was his father-in-law would impose the ban of silence. Then George might properly take him away to show him his Road, which would lead them right across the desert through the Frog Country and down to the mouth of the Queen Victoria and the people who lived there. They would meet Snake Men on the way, whom they would tell of the eventual rendezvous with the Pookarakka. Prindy would return as a Young Man. George said, 'I die finish dere, long o' my rown country. I never leave him no more . . . Goot-feller my country . . . *ngah gunga*!'

It was Prindy first saw the homestead, just a silvery flicker as of a breaking wave in the rolling violet sea that the dark line of the river timber ahead became with the climbing of the Sun. Then slowly, as if they built it in imagination as yearned they towards it over the miles of yellow dust and bleached grass and scant grey trees, it grew into a cluster of shimmering iron roofs, elevated tanks, a beef gallows, a radio mast, the darker green of alien trees.

The homestead stood in a wide clearing that would be the result of its own requirements in building material and firewood, extending on the western side of the timber of the river—Beatrice River, despite the station's name. The original homestead had stood at the confluence of the rivers, but had been too often flooded out. This place was built with the Vaisey take-over. But surely that was the original material which made up the collection of hovels on the river bank below the tanks—the blacks' camp?

Still under cover of the surrounding bush, George and Prindy came to a barbed wire fence, slipped through it, kept going till it was likely they might be seen, then turned southward. Not that there was anyone in sight to see them, as to be expected at this time of day. Even the kites and crows on the gallows seemed to be asleep. George kept on, into timber of increasing density, so that soon the homestead was lost to view. They came to another fence, passed through. Still George kept on in the same direction, southward. Beyond the fence there were outcrops of sandstone, increasing in size. At a distance of a good mile past the homestead they came upon a place amongst the rocks that was clearly a Ring Place, *Kokulal*, as George called it, putting down his things and leaning on his womera to stare about, as if seeing it in ceremonial, at length saying, 'Big trouble here before.' There was no evidence of its having been used in a long while.

'Wha' nam' trouble?' asked Prindy

George only shook his head, then picking up his things again, said, 'We go long o' river.' He set out through the rocks, now at right angles to their former course.

Over and around the rocks and thick timber they went, for about a third of a mile, with the sound of the river waxing from a murmur to a steady watery roar, to come suddenly to where the ground fell away steeply to a flat grown with grass and patches of swamp reeds and large leafy trees through which the river could be seen glinting. They went down. Horses snoozing in shade woke and stared and snorted. They crossed the flat to the river, setting down their gear to walk in through the bit of ooze along the low bank and drink deeply.

The river, some fifty yards wide, ran swift and shallow, boiling over rocks. The other bank was steep, rising to rocks and heavy timber. The shallow ran up into the glare of the Sun. It ended a little below this point, where a long green reach began steep-banked on both sides, with aquatic trees clinging, their outer roots, arching down to the water, looking like the knees of a tribe of giants sitting washing their feet.

They went from the water to a shade too low to be fouled up with horse dung, and set their things down again. Then George said he would go down to the station to see his countrymen and get those men. Prindy could do what he liked, *bogey*, perhaps; but if anybody came along, he was not to let himself be seen if possible, and if not possible, must turn his back. George slipped out of the stinking khaki shirt and trousers he had worn to rags since leaving Hang On Creek, took the shirt and ripped the back out of it, to make a square. This he slipped between his legs and knotted on each hip. He told Prindy to do likewise with his clothes, remarking, 'We properly blackfeller now...chuck-him-out clothes.' Then, carrying only his womera, he set out, heading for the tree-lined bank. A well trodden path was cut into the earth behind the trees. He followed it.

The point below the blacks' camp was well marked. Two dug-out canoes were moored to roots; and roots served as drying racks for bits of clothing; and bits of soap were stowed in crannies. Several paths ran up the bank. George went up. He stopped short of the top to stand and survey the village of hovels, dog-high for the most part, and built of any rubbish, a score or more, grouped about ash-heaped hearths, some covered with bark or tin and with cans hanging from hooks, most with a skinny dog or two beside it dead to the world. No sign of life, except swarming meat-ants. George clicked his tongue. Dogs' heads rose on the instant. Noses sniffed. One blue-heeler bitch leapt up with a growl. In an instant the place was in uproar. Black heads poked out of blackness. George, made a sign. Black bodies, most in rags, some semi-naked, all children naked, a couple of adults decently dressed if badly rumpled, came popping out. George came to the top, to strike the conventional pose of visitor, stork-like, right foot against left knee, leaning on womera. He spoke a couple of words. A shout. Several of the men came running to him. First the whiteman's greeting, the handshake, then the touching, the smoothing, the frank delight of simple people in reunion. Then a crowding round, with babble of talk, and some weeping from women. An old woman laughing toothlessly from the doorway of one of the worst of the human kennels. George went to her, bent and took her hands in one of his, and smoothed her bony arms with the other, while she mumbled and wept and then snatched a hand free to stroke him. Others stared from a distance. Some dropped down by their firesides with backs turned. Then suddenly it became dignified. All but four or five old fellows withdrew. Those remaining with George led him away towards the tank-stand, to stop and squat in the shade of the tank and talk earnestly. Others in the camp began to drift back towards the homestead.

The talk of the grey heads went on for about an hour, when two left the group to go back to their humpies, to reappear after a little while wearing nagas only and head-bands, and carrying womeras and a couple of spears and a dilly-bag apiece, and one with a sugar-sack into which he put beef hanging in chunks in one of the fire places and a hunk of bread from a hanging safe. When these two returned the rest stood up and shook hands with George, who turned away, and with the other two on his heels, went back over the bank.

Prindy came out of the shade as the trio appeared, to stand awaiting them with head hanging, sunlight glinting on recently washed hair, glowing on golden skin, The intense interest of the newcomers was evident. As they came up to him, George addressed him, in the lingo of the country, in which he must have been instructing him. Prindy looked up, causing the strangers to exclaim on intaken breath: '*Ahgorru ghuli*!' probably the equivalent to *Eh, look out*! They grey eyes surveyed them gravely.

Then George named the elders: first Kadugo, who would be daddy, and who gave his hand in the whiteman's way, then kneeling, ran both arms up the slender golden arms to the cicatrices now perfectly formed at the shoulders, smiling, murmuring, 'Properly!' then breaking into lingo,

as he brought his black hands up around jaws and ears caressing them. Prindy answered with a couple of words in lingo. 'Properly!' said Kadugo again, and rose.

The other was Ingaua—father-in-law, who for greeting turned his face sideways, as did Prindy. Neither looked directly at the other again.

Then George ushered them all into the shade, where they sat down, lit up a pipe and passed it round, the three men talking, Kadugo while he cut lines in a slice of white milkwood he had taken, along with a clasp-knife, from his dilly-bag. After a while George asked Prindy to relate what had happened at the Ring Place at Catfish Creek, that is to say the shooting, and then how the Pookarakka came to be arrested, while the strangers clicked their tongues over it. Prindy told it in Muttinglitch. By now Kadugo had his wand carved to suit his purpose, and took from his bag lumps of red and white ochre, starting with the white, moistening part of it in his mouth and then rubbing it into the engravings, after which he reddened the rest of it. This done, he tore a piece of paper-bark from the tree, and wrapped the talisman in it, bound it with a bit of fibrous grass, and handed it to Prindy with a flourish and some lingo. Again Prindy replied similarly. Then Kadugo motioned the boy to rise and go outside, and stood him with his back to the others, while he rubbed him about the head and shoulders with white ochre he had crushed in his hands and moistened with spittle, and then ran the red line down from brow to navel. Meantime, Ingaua and George slipped out from under the tree on the opposite side, and went quickly across the bit of flat and up the rocky wall, to halt at a spot amongst the rocks, from a recess in which Ingaua took a parcel, well wrapped in bark, that by its shape was a small Bull Roarer, and handed to George with a flourish and a string of words to which George replied. George placed the parcel in his own dilly-bag. Then they returned, to find Prindy painted and wearing a headband, and his daddy sitting on haunches, talking truly like father and son. The pair rose, Prindy to stand again with hanging head. Ingaua came close to the boy, and said to the others something in lingo, then placed the symbols of initiation, cane armlets and necklet of possum's fur, and with a hand on the boy's mouth pronounced the ban of silence to last till the end of his Road Following: '*Catjinga*!' Thus was renewed the *Jungara* broken by the catastrophe at Catfish.

Then George gathered up his belongings, and directed Prindy to do the same. Coming out of the shade, George shook hands with the other two. Kadugo patted Prindy on the head, while Ingaua turned away from him. Then George led the way to the tumbling water, entered it, with Prindy on his heels.

Nowhere was the stream deeper than Prindy's waist, and mostly only kneedeep, but flowing with such force that often he had to dig in his spears to keep erect or cling to rocks, and several times George had to come back to lend him a hand. Then they were across and clambering up the steep red bank. They stood a moment to look back at the pair watching from the other side. George waved, but not Prindy. The others waved. George said, '*Ngangulah*.' He swung away, headed into the tumble of rocks and twisted trees. Coming to a patch of sand, he stooped and took a handful, sprinkled some in his hair, rubbed the rest in his beard and the grey hair of his chest. He said, '*Ngah gunga* . . . my country . . . now belong 'o you country. You do all-same.' Prindy did it. George put an arm about him, chuckling, 'Properly countryman now, my *Kokanjinni*.'

Soon it was revealed that they were in a gully, with sandstone escarpments, not unlike the country back of Lily Lagoons, although the vegetation differed and the rock was brighter red. They made for a small creek running down the middle in a mass of ferns and reeds and palms, keeping to the bank above flood level for easy going. The Sun was down behind the inner wall and the sky gilding. A myriad birds were gathering for the night in the trees along the creek. A mob of white cockatoos flying over spotted the pair and wheeled back to tell everybody else that they had suspicious characters for company. Butcher birds and blue kookaburras carried on the alarm. Wallabies went crashing from the water back to the shelter of the rocks.

So on right up to the head of it, where there was a deep pool, and in the overhang above it a gallery of paintings, all sorts of figures, except the Snake. Evidently, by the blackened wall beside the pool, it was a favourite camping spot. The sky above was crimson now, fading to lilac back whence they had come. They lit a fire and grilled the beef and boiled the billy, then settled down in the soft red sand, Prindy promptly to fall asleep, while George crooned over him:

Marunga, marunga
Ma widji wa
Marunga. . . .

While man and boy were bedding down, the women and the dog dogging them were wearily coming to their chosen camp, chosen perhaps for sentimental reasons, or because they thought they might find something there they wanted, or simply because the sound emanating from it lured them on long after sunset. The sound was that of another run of rapids, at the junction of the Alice and Beatrice Rivers, grown from a murmur to a roar. On the triangle between the streams the original homestead had stood. Nell said she was 'borned dere.' It was too dark to see anything by the time they arrived, too difficult even to get to either of the rivers to drink, because in intervening ground was swampy and by the sound of it thick with cattle. After floundering into a pool they halted, drank of its pissy water, then found a bit of thicket to lie down in safety. They fell asleep to the sound of the racing waters, the crying of plovers, the bawling of the stock.

Over in the sandstone gully, the butcher birds woke the men in the silver dawn. Prindy forgot himself to the point of raising his head to mock them, but to be stopped just in time by George. Anyway, the sharp rousing got them quickly on their way. George said he wanted to see Aldinbinya burning in the first sunlight, as he had first seen it as an initiate boy being shown his Road and last as a prisoner in chains, and because it meant that the Snake was hot with rage from being stared at by his old enemy, Kurrawaddi, as they called her here, Mother of the Earth. Also, he wanted to camp within its magic tonight.

Staying only long enough to fill their bellies with water for a long dry trip over the tableland, they climbed to the top. Sure enough, out of the purple of the West, as the crimson rose behind them, there was to be seen, just as if in fact it were a giant head rising to survey the wilderness, as legend told it was in the beginning, was Aldinbinya, the Snake's Head. That was how Tchamala, during the Dreamtime bijnitch of the Frogs, had popped his head out from his subterranean realms to see how things were going.

Back at the confluence of the rivers the women were also out with first light, and by reason of starting so early on their way might well have spent the day ahead of them hungry, but for finding a bull confronting them as they made their way back to the road. Just a black bulk though he was against the silver sky, there was no doubt about his mood, the way he tossed and growled and sent the dust flying. In haste they headed back into the thicket and made their way through it, and found that it was the remains of the Chinaman's garden that had supplied the old homestead. They smelt ripe guavas, and soon found them in abundance, and also cumquats. After gorging, they filled their bags. So they went up to the road, which since they had left it had turned from westward to southward. They swung along briskly, remembering how short a distance it was, or at any rate had seemed, to the new homestead. 'Close-up,' they kept saying. 'We gitchim, Sun like o' dat,' indicating the Sun just over the trees.

But the Sun climbed up and up, while they strained ahead for the first glimpse of their objective. The flies found them, more flies than ever, because more stock, and more stock meant giving the road up to them and taking to the river timber. But cockatoos discovered them; a great gang of the snowy pests who drowned out the sound of the river with their screaming. An embarrassing situation, when they expected to see the homestead round every bend and wanted to arrive so as not to put their quarry on the run again. They were still sure that man and boy had come

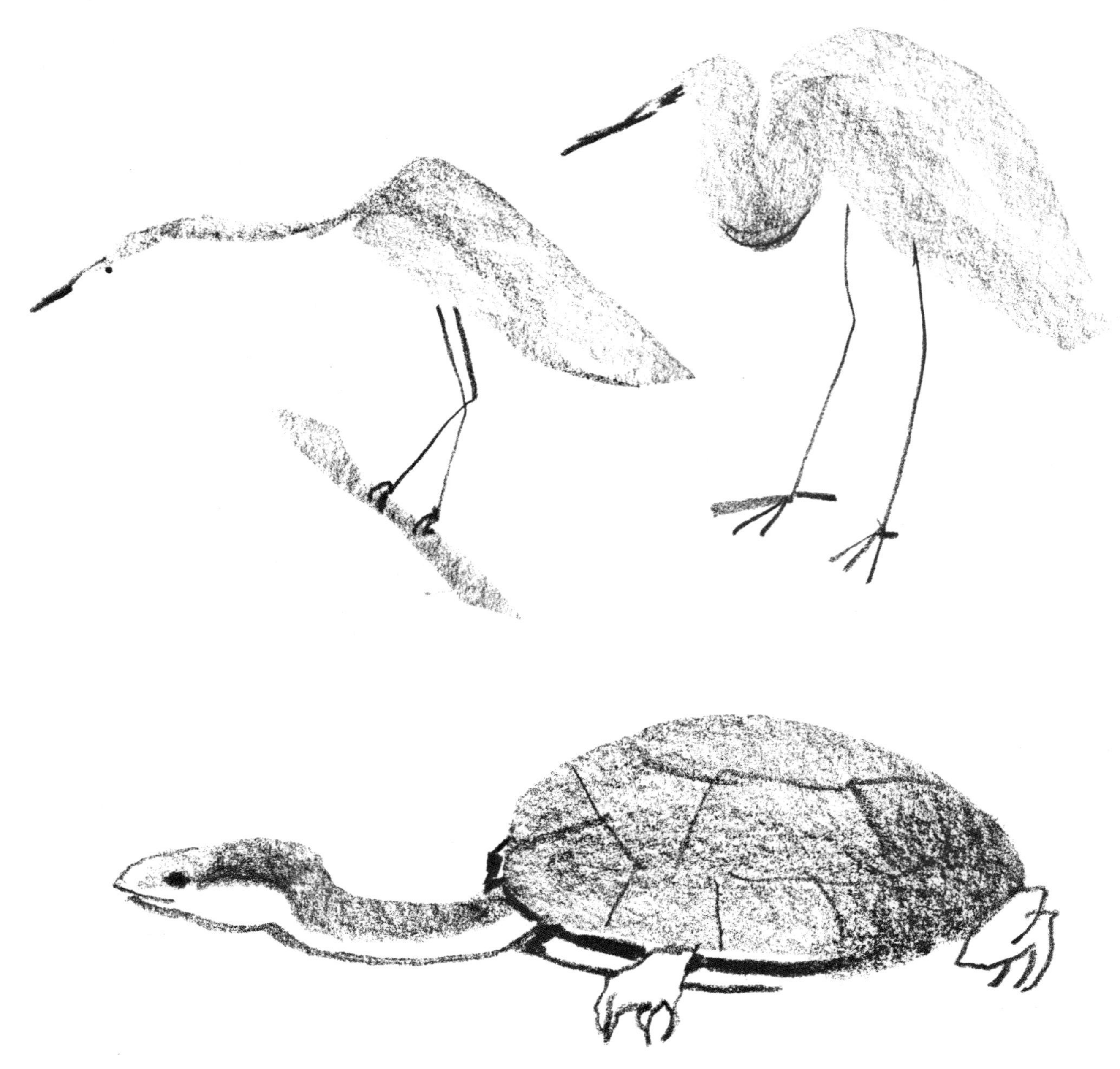

this way, by some short cut known to George. The interference of the cockatoos with their strategy forced them to sneak back across the road into the scrub on the other side and to hide till the sticky-beaks had found something better to do with their idle time. Then they got back to the road, and kept to it as much as the meandering cattle would allow. Still the Sun rose up and up, to mid-morning, past it.

Then suddenly there was a white iron gate. But as yet no other sign of civilization, except tracks inside, where cattle had not trod: horse and human and car tracks. Careful not to leave obvious tracks of their own, they got through the barbed fence, took a look at the tracks. None that they knew. Keeping off the road now, they went on, warily.

Queeny saw it first: 'Look-it!' Glimpse of the homestead through the trees.

Like those who had gone ahead of them, they intended to skirt the place unseen, deciding that if the pair were there, most likely they would be camped on that flat up-river, since that's where visitors used to stay, at least in the old times. 'Old time,' said Queeny. 'Dat mek my heart jump t'ink-about . . . dem bloody muddrin' black bastard . . . kill-him-die my man . . . close-up finish me. Look-it me now!' She panted with emotion, with crowding memories, no doubt.

Nell, staring through the trees, became aware of Mungus's tugging on the leash she held. She jerked it angrily. But he tugged, straining with sharp nose darting about the ground, and let out a yelp of protest at the restraint. Queeny hissed at him, 'Shut up!' But she was also struck by his excitement over what seemed nothing, then a little ahead of him, in a patch of soft dirt, saw what he was seeing with his nose—two plain tracks, human, of an adult and a child. 'Look-it!' she exclaimed again.

Nell bent over the small print, gasping in her excitement, 'Da's it, da's it . . . my boy . . . my boy!'

Given his head, Mungus dragged them along with a rush, whimpering softly. So through the further fence, and on, into the stone, causing Queeny to become excited: 'Sunday Place . . . dis a'way to Sunday Place . . . dat place . . . dat place . . . Oh, Jesus, oh, Jesus!'

Nell looked alarmed. They stopped, to stare ahead, while Mungus strained, whimpered. Queeny said, 'Better we go 'nother side, listen. Spone he mek bijnitch we hear him.' She meant down-wind.

So they went on again, wary now, troubled about Mungus, too, because, having been dragged away from the scent, he wanted to howl. Queeny threatened him with the crutch. Into the thick of the rocks, listening, listening; but no sound save the bluster of the wind in the stunted trees. Queeny kept whispering, 'Ring Place dere . . . dere. I know. Dis-a-way I come from homestead dat time . . . up from river flat . . . I been go . . . I been go. . . .' Her face was jerking with emotion. 'Oh, Jesus . . . deh, look out!' Mungus had found tracks again, the same tracks, of man and boy, distinct in the sand, going down towards the river.

They studied the tracks, stood debating what to do. If there were what they called a mob, they had best go and tell the station Boss. Queeny, beside herself with the old hatred now, kept saying, 'I kill him dat bastard die dis time. I don't care wha' Boss say. First chanst I get I brain him!' She swung the crutch viciously. The straining Mungus, taking fright at the movement, snatched the leash out of Nell's hand, and finding himself free, went flying through the rocks towards the river. The women looked at each other with horror. A moment. Then Nell cried, 'My boy . . . my boy dere!' She started off after the dog. Queeny called on her to wait. But she went running through the rocks.

Nell came to the steep wall, stopped, stared about the flat. The horses were there, snorting, disturbed no doubt by Mungus. Then she caught a glimpse of the little dog running round that low bush. She was starting to descend when Queeny came up, panting, 'Wha' nam'?'

Nell breathed, 'Nutching I see.'

'Wait, wait!' said Queeny. 'Might-be he sit down lil bits more far. Might-be he go long o' station camp. Betten we gitchim dog first-time. Gi' me hand get down.'

They reached the little tree to see Mungus at the water's edge. They glanced at the tracks about the tree. There was a bit of ochre and a rag of khaki. Nell snatched up the rag, smelt it. Then Mungus, looking across the rushing stream began to bark . . . *kai-kai-kai-kai*!

'Bugger dat dog!' hissed Queeny. They both started out to stop him. He came running to them barking. They grabbed him, silenced him with thumps. Squeaking he dragged them back to where he had been barking at the water's edge. There plainly in mud churned up formerly by horses going to drink were the fresh prints of man and boy, heading into the water, and depressions in the ooze, and none nearby to show that they had gone there only to drink. Mungus dragged them into the water, and standing, staring across, raised his head and howled.

Queeny said, 'Dey do 'cross dere . . . on'y two-feller.'

'We go,' said Nell.

'Might-be water too deep.'

'I don' know. I never been crost dere. Dat *wahji* place, I t'ink.'

'Da's right. I 'member. I don' care *wahji*. Jesus look out me.'

'I got 'o get back my boy.'

'I got 'o kill dat old man die.'

So they crossed, having to pick Mungus up and carry him to save him from being swept away. Over and up the other side, and onto the scent again. The cockatoos weren't there today. They must have been the gang that harassed them back along the road. On up the creek they went. The day was well on, with the Sun over the rim of the escarpment. They reached the men's camp of the night before. Tired out, they rested, but intended to climb out and go on with the hunt. However, the cockatoos came in and spotted them, and made such a din that they decided to wait till the birds settled down, lest they go with them and betray them. It was dark when they made the climb. Then the waste of rock and stunted scrub intimidated them. They found a shelter from the wind, and settled down, made a supper of guavas and cumquats, and fell asleep—if sleep it could be called, that fearful huddling together in a land of *moah*, where every rock, seen against the stars, seemed a crouching form, and the very stars in

setting over the rim of the black flatness to be taking a last look in order to report to whatever menace lurked below.

Just over that rim, in comfort and at ease as those to whom *moah* held no terrors, the two males were camped in an overhang immediately opposite Aldinbinyah, which reared its head about a mile away, measuring down the steep gully intervening and up again. As a whiteman would see it, it was the headland of another projection of this plateau, a mass of rock that for some reason had better withstood the eroding effect of the ages which had levelled most of the rest of the high country thereabout. But it was not whiteman's country, and perhaps never likely to be, so that the blackman's reasoning that it was a Shade of the Old One, Tchamala, was the proper one. Indeed, reared against a purple sky, with the swinging stars, the Cross, the Scorpion, to give it fresh eyes as the others winked out, it looked remarkably like the flat head of a serpent rampant. George and Prindy had supped on a small wallaby, a whiptail.

George told Prindy that tomorrow they must do a bit of painting in the Snake Caves over yonder. He said the Wind Spirits, to be heard humming round the Snake's Head, were on again about that trouble ahead. He couldn't make it out, since they were doing everything the Pookarakka would require of them, and were equipped to meet and pass any challenge that might be made to their going whither they were bound. However, a bit of painting might put matters right. It would certainly please the Wise One to know that his Mekullikulli had left his print here along with all the other Snake Men of the ages.

In the morning they waited to see the Snake's Head blaze back at the stare of Kurrawaddi. George said it was dangerous to be too close to Aldinbinyah when he was like that because the *moah* was too strong.

When it was safe and Aldinbinyah was just a mass of red and mauve and yellow rock, to all appearance, the pair descended into the gully. Here was a patch of rainforest, so that the sky was hidden by foliage, the ground overgrown with ferns. Orchids and staghorns hung from mossy branches. There were bushes of blackberries that George said were good eating; and they fed as they went. The trees were full of birds of many kinds. Water trickled through the mossy rocks. Aldinbinyah was completely lost to sight. It was a drop down of a good five hundred feet, into another world.

Then they began to climb and to catch glimpses of the brilliant rock, almost directly overhead, and as if looking down at them. The *moah* was very strong in here, George said. In thunderstorms the magic in the form of balls of fire rolled round the rocks. Suddenly they were out of the timber, and there was nothing but the rock. No birds up here. Even an eagle sailing down the gully was evidently keeping clear of it. Now the voices of the Wind Spirits were loud in their calling up there where round the scarlet head the very violet sky seemed whirling. So full of *moah*, so full of menace, the very air. *Oh, oh, oh*! the Spirits cried outside; and there was hollow calling back to them from the cracks and caves: *Moom, moom, moomba*!

The pair toiled upward through the rocks, where the only growth was a kind of lank spinifex, almost animalian in appearance, like spined creatures crouching. Up and up, diverging to the right, there being nothing ahead but the sheer upward curving face of the mass, the throat of the out-thrust head as it were. On the right the mass was less smooth, since eroded not simply by the south-east winds but by the north-west storms. Here at the base were overhangs. They reached the base and its comparatively level going, and halted, to rest and take the views of North and West. Mainly it was trees, trees, trees, hills at great distance: the Queen Victoria country, according to George. South-west was nothing but blue haze. There was the desert, George said, created by Tchamala when he let the water out of the great swamp where the Frog People had dwelt. They would go into the desert, see the Frog Men in rock.

They went on, turned a corner, to come suddenly upon an inward curving stretch of overhangs practically all of which even at distance could be seen to be painted galleries. George said 'Tchineke Cave number-one,' meaning that this was the chief centre of the Cult of Tchamala. Perhaps that seeming red river of painting, the serpentine coil which made the background of all such galleries and suggested that the country was bound by it from sea to sea, ended here at Aldinbinyah, The Head.

They entered the galleries. Scarcely an inch of paintable surface that was not painted, from ancient times by the look of some of the least accessible of it, but for the most part even recently. No doubt Bobwirridirridi had been here, of all places, during the brief spell of liberty he had enjoyed through the unwitting indulgence of the King of England. In fact there was his stencilled hand in every section to prove it, as George pointed out. But no tracks. No human tracks at all, only a few bird-prints and those of reptiles and wallabies and a single dingo. There were still no human tracks, because George and Prindy brush-tailed theirs away behind them. The fact that the wherewithal for painting was obviously to hand in each gallery, the pigments in the raw, brushes, grinders, and so much evidence of recent work, yet no trace of who had done it, added to the weirdness of it. Then there was that *poom, poom, poom* of the wind outside. George spoke in whispers.

There were depictions of the Wind Spirits here, fuzzy-edged circular shapes in various colours, with the usual features of representations of occult beings, the black rings of eyes connected by the loop of nose, but also having each a projection on the left-hand side, which may have been their mouths, since they were more than anything gossips and messengers. George told Prindy what they were, but had nothing to say about other paintings not the conventional ones concerned with the Cult. Perhaps these told something of the history of the Cult, evidence for such a supposition being in a pictograph showing a group of standing human male figures surrounding a prostrate female with arms and legs distorted at the joints and a large snake-like thing entering her exaggerated vulva. Since it had been touched up recently, it might well record the event in which Queeny Peg-leg had been concerned. George stared hard at it. Another that seemed to show a huge snake-mouth vomiting human figures and also recently dealt with could have told that tale of Bobwirridirridi's first dealings with the Old One. There were others, some so old as to be scarcely visible. Since George said nothing of them and yet was so eager to relate the legends of the Cult, the history might have been regarded as something unmentionable, at least in ordinary terms. No ban on speaking of Cult Men, however, George told Prindy the names of others who'd confessed themselves by leaving their hand-prints behind, one of them Jinbul. And now Prindy had to leave his. White ochre was pounded in a crude mortar and wetted with water from the billy they had brought up stopped with paper-bark. Then the paste was put in the mouth, more water added and the mixture worked on with tongue and cheeks. Then with the right hand spread against the red of the river of the Snake, the stuff was sprayed between and around the digits and down to the wrist.

They both did a little touching up in several galleries, recording the event each time with a stencil as signature. By now the morning was well advanced. George said they had better get along and bag a couple of brush-tails, one of which they must leave for the pythons of the place, else the Old One might be *koolah*. So they came out from the last of the galleries and the blue shadow cast by the head on that side, into a wild tumble of great rocks that came down like a mane from the back of the head, and beyond which, at a distance of some half a mile, began the flat eroded surface of that arm of the plateau.

They stayed amongst the rocks, listening to the *Goondalaag*, the Wind Spirits. George told Prindy to listen for directions, and sure enough, soon the boy was signalling a spot. They camped to await the appropriate time. It was easy. Out came the Marmaroo—*Zip*! *Zip*! They got one each. Prindy could offer his apologies only with silent movement of his lips: 'Poor bugger!'

The one they would leave for their mates, the *Goolgoolgabin*, must first be singed, said George, to give the python who took it a good scent for finding it. They made a small fire and did the job, then hung the dead beast up by tied feet to a rocky projection under a ledge from which only a large rearing snake could take it down and carrion birds be scared to enter. Then with the other they set out to find a place to camp on water. Water did not look likely in that blazing wilderness or rock. It would be over the

side, George said, and left it to Prindy to find it. So they followed the western rim. The Sun was fairly well down before Prindy saw and heard the signs, a cloud of little birds flitting about tree tops down about a hundred feet. They went down.

There was no sign of the water, only the smell of it and the greenery. They had to rake away leaves to find it, as a tiny well between the buttressed roots of trees, so small as scarcely to get the hand into it. A series of the little wells went down the steep hill. They drank and filled their billy, then had to look for a spot where they could camp without the risk of rolling down the hill. It was pleasant in there, out of sunlight and wind. They found their place under a shelf of rock, settled down with a fire and a feed, and watched the Sun go down over the country they would soon be going through, the desert land of the unhappy Frog Men.

Meanwhile the unhappy pursuers, following the nose of their tireless little guide, had crossed the northern arm of the plateau and come face to face, as it were, with Aldinbinyah, which even without their knowing of its *moah* troubled them so much that, although thirsty and presuming from the bird life down in the gully that water was to be had there and also food and presuming as they did that the pursuit could not lead up that sheer wall yonder but must go straight westward out across what looked like flat country, scared them so that they dared go no further that evening than the plateau's edge. The Head did not blaze an angry red for them with the sunset, but reared against the crimson sky, looked no less menacing for being purple. Queeny said of it, 'When Bible God mek de world in six day, I don' reckon he mek dat mountain. Satan mek dat-lot I reckon. No-goot place dis. No-goot all-away. Spone any goot, whiteman tek it.' Nell looked at the peak with equal distrust, but gave her attention mostly to the view straight ahead, looking for smoke, which a couple of times she thought she saw. They huddled closer than ever during the long night, while Aldinbinyah winked at them with his endless stock of eyes.

While Aldinbinyah was still black against the last of the night sky, the pair went down with their dog, found the camp of yesterday night in the overhang, and were so hungry as to vie with Mungus for the half-picked wallaby bones, sandy and anty as they were. Then on down to the water, to dally there gorging the berries and hearts of palms small enough to strip by hand—while the red *moah* glared above them. They missed it all. Again they emerged from the rainforest, toiling up the steep, it was just a huge rock they saw, even though one frightening because it looked as if ready to drop on them like a giant hand and crush them. All the while, struggling, panting, they watched it, and sighed with relief when clear of it to the right, and again when free of the labour and on the level ground of the first overhangs. But then they turned that bend and saw the galleries, and stopped dead—those who were looking, not Mungus, who, free of the leash because of the difficulty of the going and seeing not with eyes but with nose, went sniffing on. The two women breathed together: 'Eh, look out!'

Mungus went some little way, actually to the entrance to the first gallery, before realizing that he was alone. Then he turned, and yapped. The women stood rigid with terror. Then he came trotting back, whimpering, seemingly afraid that he had done something wrong. They had been able to avoid looking at the other painted galleries they had seen on the other side of the plateau, and probably realized with some special faculty that they hadn't mattered so much, anyway, as these.

Queeny breathed, 'We can't go dere.'

'Wha' we goin' 'o do?'

They viewed the alternate route round through a frightful heap of boulders, impossible for Queeny to have negotiated; or go right down to the bottom again and then climb back up when the fearsome region was by-passed. They debated it, talking of singing to Jesus to protect them as they went through, but lacked the faith. 'Somet'ing no-goot in dere, I know,' said Queeny. 'Jesus can beat anyt'ing, but not debil. Dat old debil Satan been beat' Jesus Gardener Heden. I t'ink it Satan live in dere all right. Come on, we go down.'

The descent was nearly as laborious as the climb had been, made more difficult by Mungus's dismay at being baulked, which he kept on expressing by refusing to budge and howling as he sat. The strange sound brought the birds around, amongst them some white cockatoos that made the caverns ring with their screeching. They were particularly worried because, as they

were climbing up again, they smelt smoke, just a whiff, but unmistakable.

If only they had followed their own noses then they would have spared themselves a lot of labour and time and perhaps even a great deal more; unless, in the strange circumstances Chance could be utterly ruled out. For that smoke was from the still smouldering fire on which George and Prindy had cooked a late breakfast of brush-tail before going on downhill, finished with the plateau. It was no more than a hundred yards to the right of the women's toilsome climb, that deserted camp. But for the smoke Mungus might have picked up the scent of his male friends, since the wind was blowing from there. Perhaps his nose was doing less at the moment than his memory urging him to get back to that point from which he had been snatched off the scent that had become the sole purpose of his life. He whimpered with impatience as Nell dragged on the leash to prevent his rushing madly to the top and betraying them. As if the cockatoos had not done that already to anyone on top.

Reaching the top, Mungus at once dragged them back towards the galleries, which because of the tumble of rock were not to be seen from here. They were alarmed again, but for no reason, as soon revealed by Mungus's picking up the outcoming track of the men, and turning with it, to follow them over the course they had taken in their hunt, and so eventually to where the brush-tail had been left as a gesture to the pythons. If there were any pythons about, they were too well fed just then to have bothered with the gift. It still hung there, and not in any way to scare the hungry ones who viewed it now, because the tracks they knew so well were beneath it. The dead beast seemed to be quite fresh. Not more than half a dozen bluebottles were on it. The women did express wonder at why it had been hung like that, and for a moment looked about doubtfully. But hunger got the better of them. Queeny hooked it down with her crutch. They built up a fire on the spot where the wallaby had been smoked, and hacked the meat up with flints they had already gathered, and soon were gorging. Exhausted as well as replete with food they slept, slept long. The Sun was well down before they woke.

But this was no place to camp, even if they had time to tarry. They must have water. On they went again—and down, and found how close they had been to accomplishment of their mission. In fact they believed that the men must have been there when they passed, because the fire was only just dead when they reached it. Therefore, after drinking deeply and filling their can, they went on down. But night fell on them in dense forest. They had to stop. Still in sight of Aldinbinyah, who with ruddy countenance in the last light, seemed very definitely to be watching them.

George's determination for that same day was to get through the forest country below the plateau, and travelling South of West, make camp on a waterhole he called *Gubbindah Wiyan*, which was on the stony edge of the Frog Country. It went to plan. With the Sun on the one horizon, and Aldinbinyah as a ruddy spot on the other, they came out of the thinning timber into a region of great pinkish grey slabs of rock that lay like giant's paving, gently sloping to red infinity, it seemed. Mostly only small bushes and spinifex grew from the cracks; but here and there, standing starkly against the sunset, were so-called bottle trees, *Bamgulut*. Water was obtainable from a bottle-tree, of course, as George would show Prindy, who was now looking on the odd things for the first time; but the water they wanted was from a *gubbindah*, which meant a gecko. In many places throughout the rocks, according to George, were these holes, which led down to the great river through which Tchamala made his way about his nether world. Each was guarded by a *gubbindah*. Only certain. creatures favoured by the Old One, amongst them Snake Men, might drink. If others tried, the gecko in charge would call in his tiny voice, which became thunder down below; whereupon the Old One would suck the water back, and the intruder with it. One of the favoured was *Bilbilgah*, the Night Parrot of the desert country, who kept a look-out for Tchamala during the night and always reported to a *gubbindah* before dawn, when the flock went for the one drink they had from dawn till dawn of each day. The easiest way to find a *gubbindah* hole was to listen for the parrots coming to drink, because they made a lot of noise about it. However, failing that, you could

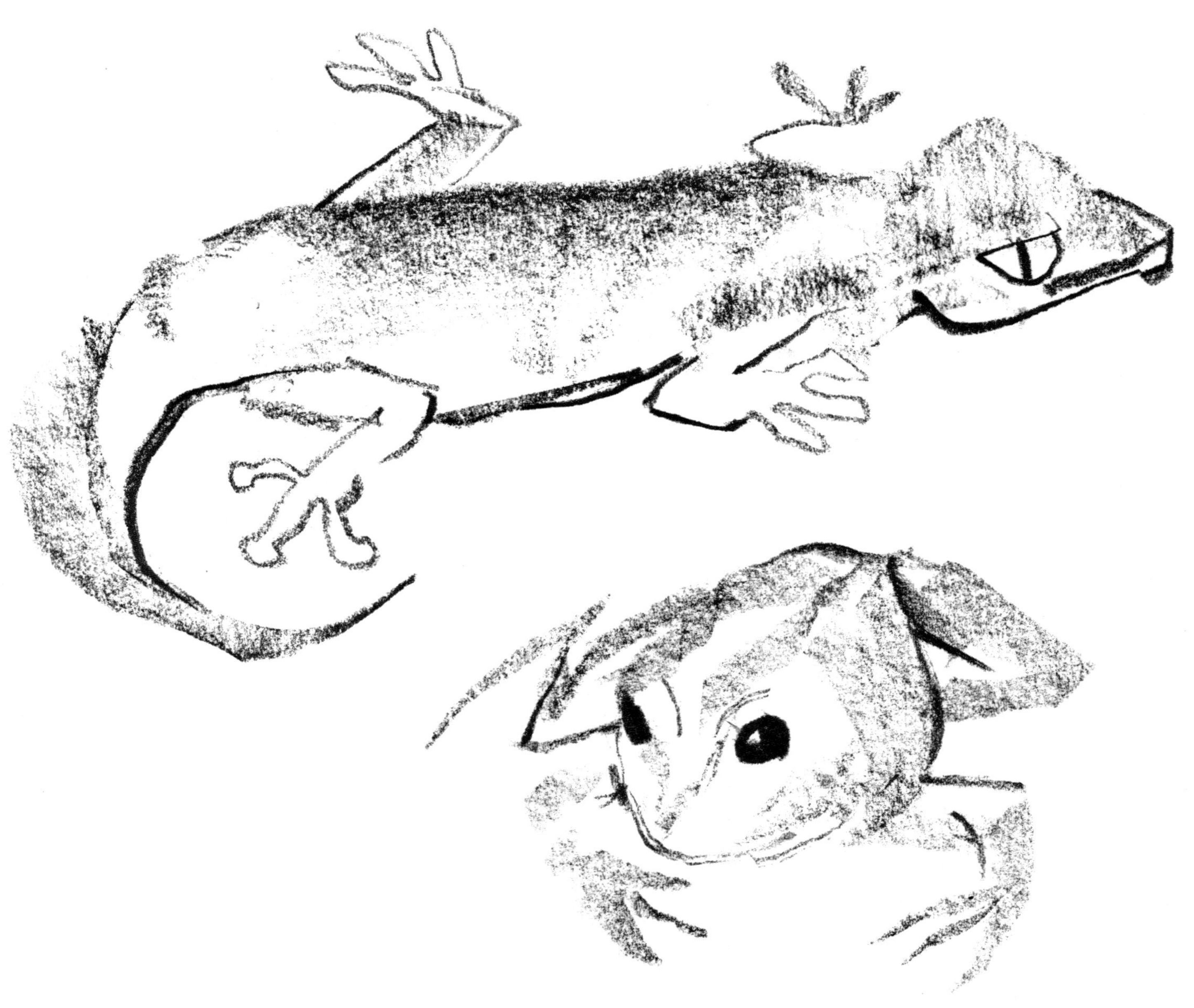

pick out the spot by their *goona* on the rock. Because there was magic in the droppings you could see them in the dark. They would go look-about.

In this case, as so often, the blackman's idea of the geological history of the locality fairly fitted the whiteman's, while being so much more picturesque. Undoubtedly here had been a great lake, of which the mass of flat cracked sedimentary rock had been the bed. George's full story of its origin was that the Ol'Goomun-Ol'Goomun had made the great swamp for the Beral People, the Frogs. Living according to the rules she had taught them, the Beral had been as happy as the frogs of today are when the rains come, singing all day and all night long. Then Tchamala had come along and asked them what sort of life was it when you did the same thing all the while. The Beral asked him how to break the monotony. He said, simply by breaking those crazy rules—do a bit of *tchinekin* now and again. But the Beral, who were giants, did their *tchinekin* in such a big way that it led to a battle royal. Koonapippi (or Kurrawaddi) came along to stop it. Then it was that Tchamala made a hole in the swamp from underneath, so that all the water ran out into his river. The Beral perished. Prindy would see their Shades in rock away over there where the sand was. The swamp frogs of today, called *Gulladulla*, were a new lot made by the Ol'Goomun. She fixed it with them so that they would never go Wrong Side like the Beral. They didn't have husbands and wives like other creatures. The females simply laid their eggs; and the males came along and had a big corroboree to show that they were happy with the arrangement. But what a life, as the Old One had said so long ago!

The *Bamgulut*, the bottle-trees, said George, were people in the Beginning, the ancestors of the yam called *Miyakka*. They'd been mixed up in the great fight of the Beral, but had more sense than the Frogs in filling themselves with water before it disappeared. They were able to show a few of the Beral the trick in time, but very few, and these shrunk to mere handfuls. However, they continued to exist, and were to be found still, dug deep in the sand of the desert and came in handy if you were perishing for a drink; although you had to be a desert blackfellow to find them.

They went on out over the baked remains of the paradise that had been, carrying a few sticks of wood with them from the forest, and also a bagful of *larrama*, the pods of the so-called Kapok, the seeds of which make good eating roasted. Dark descended. It seemed a hopeless venture, searching for water there; and probably it was; but according to George they were not searching, but being called by a *gubbindah*, even if in a voice so tiny that it could not be heard. Sure enough, there at last in the darkness was a faint glowing. They headed for it. Spinifex grew profusely here between the rocks. George rolled a bundle of it about a stick to make a torch, lit it with a match. There was a widish space between slabs and a concavity beneath one of them. You had to crawl to get in; but inside was quite a cave, with a little hole in the bottom that showed the glint of water. And there, coming out of a crack in the wall ahead was a little white gecko, with bulging black eyes that flashed fire, challenging them in a tiny voice: *Gekk-gekk-gee*! George replied in lingo, at such length that the torch died. But the gecko remained glowing. *Gekk-gekk-gee*! the gecko said—and no doubt about it, a rumbling echo from below! George bent down to fill the billy. Prindy, behind him, stared. Then as George turned, Prindy backed out. They got into another hollow between slabs and built their fire and made their bedding-down places.

The wind moaned across the wilderness of rock. George said several times, 'I don' like it wha' dat-lot talk-talk. I can't-mek-it-out . . . but I don' like it.' Again he sang quietly to himself for hours while his small companion slept.

The night parrots woke them in coming to water, swooped over and around them in a twittering cloud dark against the stars, then went to water, evidently learnt from the gecko that all was in order, because, sitting the white rock while taking turns at the water, they were silent. Then, like a puff of smoke against the paling eastern sky, they were gone. George said that they dwelt in other caves in the ground during daylight, scared of coming out till dark, because the Ol'Goomun, for whom, like all the cocky species, they had been scouts in the Beginning, would blind them with that eye of hers, the Sun, for having betrayed her at the time of the Frog People bijnitch, by not reporting to her what Tchamala was doing with the waters of the swamp. It was because of this connexion with the Old One that they were permitted to drink of the secret waters.

After eating up the rest of their larrama seeds, they went down again to the water, filled their bellies to bursting for a long and perhaps waterless leg and took leave of little Gubbindah, the custodian, who duly came out of his crack and spoke. Then away again, west-south-westward.

The westward fall of the rocky waste was perceptible, but only just. That is in looking ahead. To look back was to see what looked like a purple mountain range, growing in size as they went, sometimes, as the Sun got up and mirage rolled everywhere, seeming even to be pushing after them. George said he didn't like it, that it might be a warning from the wind spirits that there were enemies behind. But who could be behind there? And what enemies could they have, now they were out of whitefellow country and had full warranty for passage through this domain of their own kind?

They came to another *gubbindah wiyan* just before noon, and went below to pay their respects to the keeper and drink their fill. Here was the beginning of the end of the region of flaggy rock. A short way off it ended suddenly, to become a red plain, timbered with the dwarf tough stuff of deserts, the gidjia, wilga, mulga, with here and there a bottle-tree looking over the tops of the others with tiny branches making them appear rather like old-men kangaroos taking stock of things. This was the proper Frog Country, George said. Soon they would see the petrified Frog Men. They went on. The earth they trod now was not merely red, but a mixture of reds of every hue, not merely mixed, but in streaks and patches, comprised of tiny polished granules that glistened so that every one might be an opal or an agate, heaped up, some of it, in large purplish mounds that were the nest of meat ants, the only ground creatures, apparently, to inhabit the waste.

Then suddenly there were the Frog Men peeping, blue humps in the distance: one, two, three. George named them: Karra Beral, the Boss, Barra Beral, Binga Beral. Then a whole horde peeping. Prindy, by his nodding head, was silently counting them, in the way of the *kuttabah*: around thirty. How would the *kuttabah* in his cleverness account for thirty large chunks of rock standing in the midst of a terrain where nothing else in stone was larger than a grain of rice?

The rocks reddened as approached, and took on very much the shape of squatting frogs, with heads all turned in the same direction: north-west. George said they were facing that way in expectation of the rain that at last would come to break their long long limbo. The rocks occupied an area of about half a mile square, the vegetation of which, although similar to that of the rest of the plain, was of much denser and bigger growth. There were numerous bottle-trees, all carved with Aboriginal symbols, and kapok trees galore on the pods of which hordes of green lorikeets, hanging upside down and looking like half-ripe fruit themselves, were feasting. The lorries saw them and rose up in alarm, but settled down when it appeared that the intruders were not interested in them. George said they would bag what they wanted when good and ready. The birds would have to home to water, he said, a long way from here, on one of the heads of the Queen Victoria. He jerked his jaw west-north-westward. They would stop eating and sit preening a while before they took off in a flock. While eating they were watchful, like all other creatures. Preening they would be preoccupied, only waiting for the leader's signal. That would be the time to get them, each to find a bunch perched together, and simultaneously to put boomerangs into them. Meantime they would make camp under one of the bigger rocks, would get water from a bottle-tree, and collect *pituri*, which grew under the rocks, and which George had not had a whiff of in too long.

They chose Binga Beral whose belly was painted with many designs, but none concerned with the Snake. George got his *pituri* and made a cigarette of it and smoked happily, till he had to put it down, saying it made him drunk. He soon recovered. Then they went to get water. The trees were all bored, with plugs in the holes. It was like drinking from a tap, only something much more refreshing than water, slightly sweet yet tart to taste. 'Goot-feller, eh?' asked George. He often asked sudden questions like that, as if to catch the novice, but had not done so yet. Prindy smiled his appreciation.

They made a fire and gathered kapok pods knocked down by the lorikeets and put them on to roast. Then they sneaked out for the kill, came back with a round dozen of the lovely creatures, their emerald plumage crimsoned with their blood. The rest fled shrieking for their far-off home on water.

About the same time, those enemies of whose pursuing George had divined and yet forgotten, reached the bottom of that seeming purple wall and with the nose of Mungus found the secret water-holes and drank from them without incurring the wrath of Tchamala, even though watched by the geckos, and warned by the thunder below. They had moved fast, believed they were right on the heels of those they sought, but were intimidated by the red wilderness ahead in the red evening, and gave up.

There as the light faded from the sky was to be seen the newborn Igulgul, just hanging above the heads of those seeming ever-watchful old-men kangaroos. Queeny said, 'New Moon for luck. You wish for sumpin. Den I turn over my money, for mek more. Go on . . . wha' nam' you wish?'

Nell murmured: 'I wish I find my boy tomorro', and all dis no-goot bijnitch finish.'

'I wish all-same, on'y I wan' 'o gi' dat bloody black bastard hidin' so he go 'way die . . . pug him! Den I wan' go Beatrice River Races . . . and you 'n me mek pie and sell him and mek plenty money.' She took the sweaty roll of notes from her drawers, and staring at the ghostly sliver of silver, solemnly turned it over, muttering, 'For Jesus Crise sake, hay-men!'

George squatting with Prindy under the painted red belly of Binga Beral, watching young Igulgul vanish with what looked like a sly wink hinting of lively Wrong Side things to watch for during his coming season, remarked to Prindy that the trouble he felt convinced was imminent might come from blackfellows away over where those lorikeets had gone. These would know that the birds had been disturbed, perhaps find a couple wounded amongst them, and think strangers were about and lay ambush for themselves, if they didn't do something about it. He reckoned that it would be a good idea to put up a smoke signal tomorrow, three smokes to show that they were coming in peace. They would gather up fuel first thing in the morning.

But Igulgul was in this, apparently, with his power over the Winds and his perversity. Starting with the dawn, they had three nice piles of smoke-producing stuff laid out about half a mile apart and all ready for the match, when the morning breeze that could be expected with the rising of the Sun, began to bluster, surely at the instigation of the invisible sly one just then taking to the eastern sky. It would have been useless to light the fires for the purpose designated, because the smoke would simply have poured as one stream and scarcely above the level of the ground. George said they would wait for the lull that might be expected at midday, and meantime would look around, do a bit of carving on the bottle-trees, and gather a quantity of *pituri* as a gift to those they were going to and have some in hand for the Pookarakka when he came along, he being very partial to it.

It was getting close to noon, and the wind dropping as expected, and George and Prindy back in the screened shade of Binga Beral, George singing softly, while Prindy gently clicked two boomerangs—when Prindy's hands stopped suddenly, his head cocked. George breathed, 'Wha' nam'?' The answer came from outside, scuffling, snuffling. Both grabbed for weapons: but before they could rise, they were overwhelmed by Mungus, flopping all over them, yapping his delight: *Kai-kai-kai-kai-kai-kai-kai*!

George flung the dog off, leapt up, ran crouching to the northern corner where Mungus had entered, stopped to peer through the screening bushes. Some fifty yards away, plain to see amidst the sparse vegetation, Nell stood, with her bundles, staring at the rock. He looked quickly elsewhere. No sign of anyone else. Nell dropped her load, but carrying a length of wood, began to approach. George breathed to Prindy at his elbow, '*Ngah pooropooro*.' Prindy fell back.

George fixed a spear to his womera, stepped outside. Nell stopped at sight of him. He gave another swift glance round, then looking at her, demanded, 'Wha' you want?'

She called hoarsely, 'Where my boy?'

'He all right. Wha' you doin' here? Dis place *tjungara*. Who been come long o' you?'

'Nutching. I wan' my boy.'

'By'n'by you get him. Now you git.

She started towards him again. He raised the spear: 'I tell him you dis place *tjungara*. I let you have him spear you come more close-up.'

She shrieked, 'I wan' my boy... I wan' my boy.... Boy, boy, where you, boy?'

Prindy, inside, clicked his tongue. George ignored him, aiming the spear as if to hurl it, yelling, 'No more gammon... I kill-him-you-die, woman, spone you come more close-up!'

She stopped again. It wasn't on account of his mother that Prindy had given the signal. There within ten yards, to the left, was Queeny, emerged from behind a bottle-tree, taking aim at George with a length of wood in shape somewhat like a boomerang. Prindy clicked urgently. But it was Mungus who drew George's attention to the danger, by shooting out with a delighted yap to greet another old friend, one from whom probably he'd been forcibly parted not so long ago in order to effect just this strategy.

George looked just too late. As he swung the spear, the rough weapon came whirling towards him. He raised the spear to ward it off. But it was too heavy and the force behind it too great. It snapped the spear, and in doing so, veered up and struck him fair in the face, where otherwise it might have hit him in the belly.

George staggered, fell in a heap with his other spears. Yelling at the top of her powerful contralto, Queeny came in with her crutch: 'You bloody puggin black muddrin bastard, I got you now!' *Whack, whack*! The heavy crutch-leg smote his head. George rolled over, was taking it on the back of the head, when Mungus, yapping protest against this falling out of his friends, leapt into it took the most savage of the blows, howled and rolled over kicking. It gave George time to grab his big shovel spear, to roll into a sitting posture, and from there to drive it past the crutch rising again to deal with him, into the fat belly behind it. Queeny screamed, lost balance, fell on her back.

But there was Nell now charging in with her lump of wood, shrieking inarticulate in fearful rage, but to swing away as George snatched up another spear. George raised the spear without womera to aim, shouting, 'No-goot bloody halfcaste woman . . . you break him *tjungara* . . . you die finish . . . .'

Prindy leapt out, crying his first utterance in days, a croaked, 'Oh . . . no-more like o' dat!'

But the spear was on its way. Nell, now with back turned, took it between the shoulder blades. She screamed, flung up her arms, staggered a few steps, then fell flat on her face, with hands and feet beating the red earth, the upright spear haft swinging like a pendulum in reverse. Prindy staring great-eyed, glanced at a movement from goggling gasping Queeny, to see her pull the spear from her belly and a gout of blood follow it. George also turned, and as she struggled to her knees, gasping at him, 'Black bastard you die now!' bent to get another spear. But too late again. She caught him in the left side, driving the head of the spear out of sight up under his ribs. He coughed, fell sideways with blood gushing from his mouth. He looked at Prindy, raised his hand as if to make some peremptory sign—then fell on his back, mouth and eyes wide.

Queeny got her crutch, heaved herself up with it, stood over George, gasping, 'You daid, all right, old-man . . . now we square.' She turned to look at Nell, stared a moment, then swung towards her, reached her in a few long swinging strides, while clutching with a hand at her own bleeding belly. She bent over her, saw one eye glaring, bloody tongue fallen in the dust, and stood erect and howled like a dingo: 'Oh, oh, ow, ai-ee!' Then with her bloodied hand she tore at her own hair, tearing strands out of it, crying, 'Oh, my tchister, my lil tchister . . . daid, daid . . . she be daid . . . Oh, Jesus save my lil tchister . . . oh, oh, ah, ai-ee! I no-more been do it, tchister . . . I didn'

done it.' She smote her own head hard.

She turned to look at Prindy, who was staring open-mouthed from one to other of those who had died so swiftly, as if he didn't believe it. Mungus was dead, with bloody tongue also in the dust and red meat-ants already at work on it. Prindy looked at Queeny, at the bloody mess below her waist. She gasped at him: 'You got him water?' He nodded. She licked her lips, adding, 'I thirsty too much. Gi' me drink.' He went in under the rock, came out with the billy that had been filled at a bottle-tree. She drank greedily. She muttered, 'I too hot. Wan' 'o sit . . . wan' 'o sit shade.'

She swung towards the rock. He looked alarmed, raised his hand in a sign of stop. 'Wha's matter you no-more talk?' she asked, and when he put his hand to his nose in the sign that he was bound to silence, she snorted, 'Blackfeller rubbitch. You talk my boy . . . you talk me!' She went into the shade, while he stared wide-eyed at her temerity. She let herself down slowly, moaning with pain, back to the rock, staring out upon the fearful scene. 'Muddrin bijnitch,' she muttered. 'I been dream dat, ain't it . . . dream about black flyin' fox. Gi' me more water, my boy. Oh, my tchister, poor daid feller . . . I didn't done it, my tchister . . . oh, ai-eeee!'

When she had drunk, she said, 'You 'n me got 'o go p'lice.'

When he looked his opposition, she added querulously, 'Got 'o go gitchim p'liceman. Muddrin bijnitch no-goot. Dis 'Preme Court bjinitch. We got 'o go back Alice Station . . . oh, ah!' She fainted.

Prindy stood staring still: at his mother over there with the ants swarming over her dark side-turned face: at George with ants at his eyes, and the caked mass of blood about his side: at Mungus, so thick with them that they seemed to be moving him away.

Queeny recovered, croaked, 'Water . . . water . . . I thirsty too much.' She finished the can.

Prindy looked around again, then went off, past the rock, to a big bottle-tree, where he pulled a plug and let the fluid trickle in. There was his fresh cut in the bulbous trunk, a design dictated by George as a memento of his novitiate, so many marks for each moon of his Road Following, and only one so far. He took a long swig himself. Then when the billy was filled he returned with it, but slowly, with evident reluctance.

The scene was the same. He looked at it as if he'd been wishing it to be different. Queeny, in a weak voice, scolded him for being away so long, and hogged the water. She said they couldn't leave his mother like that; they must try to drag her in here and cover her up. He shook his head, and when she waxed querulous about blackfeller bijnitch, went off with his tommy-axe

and cut branches from bushes, and gingerly went to his mother, and covered her. Then he went to do the same to George, and persisted with it, even while Queeny scolded, 'Let dem ant eat dat bloody puggin old bastard... Satan goin' 'o get him, burn, him long o' down-below.' She went on, rambling somewhat: 'Jesus goin' 'o look out my tchister... you mumma... Jesus love me, yest I know... de Bible tell me so....'

Streams of ants were coming from everywhere, and to such activity that the leaves of the shrouding branches could be heard rustling to it. Queeny complained of feeling sleepy, and lay down. Prindy had to get more water for her, and hold up her head to help her drink it. She murmured that she would be all right after she'd had a sleep. She told him how she had crawled to the station homestead that time with broken legs and busted belly. 'Nobody can kill me daid,' she said. 'Cos Jesus love me....'

Prindy went off to get kapok pods, having to climb for them today, since no lorikeets came back to drop them. Then he made a fire and cooked them, and tried to get Queeny to eat. She had little to say now. Mostly she slept. If she woke and he were there, she would look at him and smile and whisper, 'Lil Lord Jesus.'

The Sun went down on the other side of the rock. Igulgul went down, without being able to see how things were, but no doubt knowing all about it. Night parrots flew over, and came back to take a look, perhaps to report in the morning to their gekko on what had happened to those two intruders who'd made bold to drink the waters of the elect. Tchamala always got 'em, one way or another.

As night fell and Queeny complained of cold and that was the windy eastern side, she asked to be helped in under the rock, but didn't abuse him when he made no move to do so. She and Nell had brought their sacking with them. He covered her with the lot. Then he got into the cavity himself and dug into the sand.

Often Queeny woke him, calling for water. He went to her. Then a last time, but this time the call was to Jesus, whom she showed to him on the horizon: 'All dress' white... look-it... sweet Jesus....' It was the Pleiades, the Ol'Goomun-Ol'Goomun's form of nights, probably the first appearance of the Constellation for the season, because the dawn was near, as witness the passing clouds of parrots. Then she got her religions mixed and babbled of Jesus and the Ol'Goomun as the one. 'Ol'Goomun Jesus,' she sighed. 'You look-out we. We foller him you. All-away we foller him you... Mumma-Ol'Goomun-Jesus....' Then she fell silent.

Prindy, sitting near, watched the Ol'Goomun, who indeed seemed to be beckoning as she climbed the sky. She didn't get far before that part of her universal self faded with the dawning of that other self, the Sun. Prindy didn't have to wait for the Sun to come up to find that he was the sole survivor of whatever bit of devilry had led to the massacre. The ants, not out of the holes yet, hadn't started on Queeny; but there was no doubt about her being what he would call *warriji jeega*, completely dead. He took one long look at her, then went and got his things together, his own things only. These he took a little way off, then returning, with his brush-tail, he circumscribed the scene with a wide band of erasion that would be designed to prevent the Shades of the dead following him and making a nuisance of themselves, as the newly dead had a tendency to do. Then he set off, south-westward, as he had been going with George, and after covering only fifty yards or so, began to whimper and beat his head with a boomerang, muttering, 'I no-more been do it, daid-feller...no-more me...no-more me....' For just a little while. Then quite quickly he sniffed back his tears, and in doing so, began to swing more south-ward, more and more, till he was travelling due South, heading for just such a purple wall as the day before yesterday he and George had left behind them. In mid-morning he reached the foot of it, and went on over the slabs, before long to come to one of those white patches and go down to see the gecko and get a drink. It was cool in there. Perhaps it was a dangerous place to tarry. But he'd had little sleep the night before, and who knew how much emotional stress. He fell asleep.

He was wakened by the gecko, standing on hind legs close to him and most likely telling him to be on his way. He drank deeply and went out. It was well past noon. Whether he did so aimlessly or because the sunlight was fierce and best turned full away from and the wind was fresh in his face, or from some deeper urge than any but the like of him would know, now he headed eastward. Night caught him still on the flaggy rocks. He got into a hollow, and watching Igulgul watching him, fell asleep.

He woke in the morning to find the Ol'Goomun beckoning from the eastern horizon. He gathered up his things and went obediently.